CONTENTS

Introduction

Citizenship and National Identity is the one hundred and thirty-first volume in the **Issues** series. The aim of this series is to offer up-to-date information about important issues in our world.

Citizenship and National Identity looks at the issues of national identity and notions of 'Britishness', voting and government in the UK and the role of citizenship in the lives of young people.

The information comes from a wide variety of sources and includes:
Government reports and statistics
Newspaper reports and features
Magazine articles and surveys
Website material
Literature from lobby groups
and charitable organisations.

It is hoped that, as you read about the many aspects of the issues explored in this book, you will critically evaluate the information presented. It is important that you decide whether you are being presented with facts or opinions. Does the writer give a biased or an unbiased report? If an opinion is being expressed, do you agree with the writer?

Citizenship and National Identity offers a useful starting-point for those who need convenient access to information about the many issues involved. However, it is only a starting-point. Following each article is a URL to the relevant organisation's website, which you may wish to visit for further information.

* * * * *

Citizenship and National Identity

ISSUES

Volume 131

Series Editor

Lisa Firth

 *Independence*

Educational Publishers
Cambridge

First published by Independence
PO Box 295
Cambridge CB1 3XP
England

© Independence 2007

British Library Cataloguing in Publication Data
Citizenship and National Identity – (Issues Series)
I. Firth, Lisa II. Series
323.6

ISBN 978 1 86168 377 9

Printed in Great Britain
MWL Print Group Ltd

Cover
The illustration on the front cover is by
Angelo Madrid.

Citizenship and belonging

What is Britishness?

What is Britishness?

Most of the research participants shared a common representation of Britishness, ranging over eight dimensions:

⇨ Geography: Britishness was associated with the British Isles, and with typical topographic features, such as the Scottish Highlands, lochs, Welsh valleys, and rolling hills.

⇨ National symbols: Britishness was symbolised by the Union Jack and the royal family.

⇨ People: Three different ways of thinking about the British people emerged: for some participants, the British included all British citizens (that is, those who hold UK passports), regardless of region or ethnicity; for others, the British were exclusively associated with white English people; and for others still, the British included people of very diverse ethnic origins.

⇨ Values and attitudes: These included upholding human rights and freedoms, respect for the rule of law, fairness, tolerance and respect for others, reserve and pride (generally valued by white English participants and criticised by white Scottish and white Welsh participants, as well as those from ethnic minority backgrounds), a strong work ethic, community spirit, mutual help, stoicism and compassion, and drunkenness, hooliganism and yobbishness.

⇨ Cultural habits and behaviour: These included queuing; watching and supporting football, cricket and rugby; and consuming food and drink such as 'fish and chips', 'English breakfast', 'Yorkshire pudding', 'cream teas', 'cucumber sandwiches', 'roast beef', 'Sunday lunch', 'curries' and 'beer'.

⇨ Citizenship: For Scottish and Welsh participants, and for most participants from ethnic minority backgrounds, Britishness was very much associated with holding a UK passport. This was not salient among white English participants.

⇨ Language: English was seen as a common language that unites the British people. The array of British accents (in terms of regional and class differences) was also seen as typically British.

⇨ Achievements: Britishness was associated with political and historical achievements (the establishment of parliamentary democracy, empire and colonialism); technological and scientific achievements (the industrial revolution, medical discoveries); sporting achievements (the invention of many sports); and 'pop' cultural achievements.

Identification with Britishness

While the content of 'Britishness' was shared across most groups, there were important differences in the ways in which participants personally related to, and identified with, Britishness.

As UK passport holders, all the participants knew they were British citizens, but not everyone attached any value significance to being British. In Scotland and Wales, white and ethnic minority participants identified more strongly with each of those countries than with Britain. In England, white English participants perceived themselves as English first and as British second, while ethnic minority participants perceived themselves as British; none identified as English, which they saw as meaning exclusively white people. Thus, the participants who identified most strongly with Britishness were those from ethnic minority backgrounds resident in England.

Ethnic minority participants also drew on other sources of identification: religion (for Muslims only); ethnicity (region, country or continent of origins, and their associated cultures); and race or colour (for black Caribbean and black African participants only). These various identities became more or less salient in different situations. They were seen as being compatible with Britishness.

October 2005

⇨ Information extracted from the Commission for Racial Equality's report *Citizenship and Belonging: What is Britishness?*, conducted and written by ETHNOS for the CRE, and reprinted with permission. Visit www.cre.gov.uk for more information or to view the full report.

The citizenship survey 2005

Information from the Department for Communities and Local Government

⇨ 80 per cent of people in England and Wales feel that they live in a cohesive community, in that they agree that their local area is a place where people from different backgrounds get on well together. This proportion is unchanged from 2003.

⇨ 53 per cent of people whose friends are all the same ethnicity as themselves feel that racial prejudice in Britain has got worse over the last five years, compared to 43 per cent of people who have friends from different ethnic groups.

⇨ In England and Wales, 37 per cent of people from minority ethnic groups feel they would be treated worse than other races by at least one of eight public service organisations. This proportion is unchanged from 2001.

⇨ 39 per cent of people in England feel they can influence decisions in their local area, 22 per cent feel they can influence decisions at a national level.

⇨ Half (50 per cent) of adults in England volunteered regularly in the past year. This has increased from 2001 (47 per cent).

The survey monitors elements of the Government's race equality and cohesion target, 'to reduce race inequalities and build community cohesion'. This target also includes perceptions of discrimination in the labour market. The survey is also used to monitor part of the target relating to building confidence in the criminal justice system (owned by Home Office) and part of the volunteering target (owned by the Office of the Third Sector in the Cabinet Office).

---

83 per cent of people who live in areas containing people from different ethnic groups felt that in their area people respected ethnic differences

---

The surveys cover a range of topics which include: views about the local area; racial and religious prejudice and discrimination; active community participation; civil renewal and social networks. Detailed results from the 2005 survey are published today in a series of four reports. More detail of key findings follows:

Community cohesion

Overall, 80 per cent of adults feel that they live in a cohesive community, where people from different backgrounds get on well together. Asian, Black and Chinese people are more likely than Mixed race and White people to feel that they live in a cohesive community.

83 per cent of people who live in areas containing people from different ethnic groups felt that in

their area people respected ethnic differences. This has increased from 2003 (79 per cent).

Race and faith

People who live in multi-ethnic areas and those with friends from different ethnic groups to themselves tend to have the most positive views about racial prejudice in Britain. 31 per cent of those who live in areas with the highest density of minority ethnic households (top decile) feel there is more racial prejudice today, compared to 48 per cent overall.

People from minority ethnic groups are much less likely to feel that racial discrimination has got worse in Britain over the last five years than White people. 31 per cent of people from minority ethnic groups felt that there is more racial prejudice now, compared to 50 per cent of White people (48 per cent overall). In terms of age, younger people (16-24) were the most positive (35 per cent).

One element of the Government's race equality and cohesion target is to reduce the percentage of people from minority ethnic groups who feel they would be treated worse than people of other races by one or more public service organisations. This figure in 2005 was 37 per cent, which has not changed significantly from the 2001 figure.

Between 2001 and 2005 the percentage of people from ethnic minorities who feel that they would be treated worse than other races by the police has improved, from 27 per cent in 2001 to 24 per cent in 2005. There has also been an improvement for the prison service (21 per cent down to 17 per cent), the Courts (14 per cent down to 12 per cent) and the Crown Prosecution Service (14 per cent down to 11 per cent).

Among people from minority ethnic groups who said they had been treated unfairly at work regarding promotion or progression, half (50 per cent) felt it was for reasons of race.

20.4 million adults in England (50 per cent) volunteered regularly in the 12 months before interview

Among people from minority ethnic groups who had been refused a job in the last five years, 22 per cent said it was because of their race.

A quarter (24 per cent) of people feel there is 'a a lot' of religious prejudice in Britain, with about half (52 per cent) feeling levels of religious prejudice have increased over the last five years.

Among people who feel that racial prejudice has increased, there was a marked increase in the proportion citing Muslims as a group experiencing more prejudice (37 per cent in 2005, compared to 17 per cent in 2003).

Active communities

20.4 million adults in England (50 per cent) volunteered regularly in the 12 months before interview. This was an increase on the 18.4 million adults who had volunteered in 2001.

The Government's volunteering target focuses on increasing voluntary activity by individuals at risk of social exclusion, defined as people with no qualifications, with a disability or limiting long-term illness or from a minority ethnic group. The overall rate for regular volunteering among this group was 43 per cent.

About four out of five people in England (78 per cent) gave money to charity in the four weeks before interview, with buying raffle tickets being the most often cited method.

47 per cent of people in England had participated in a civil renewal activity in the last year. This covers a spectrum of activity from signing a petition or taking part in a public demonstration, through to involvement in decision-making about local services.
27 June 2006

⇨ The above information is reprinted with kind permission from the Department for Communities and Local Government. Visit www.dclg.gov.uk for more information.
© Crown copyright

The union jack – a symbol of unity or division?

Information from the Economic and Social Research Council

I t's 400 years old today (12 March), but four centuries on, the union jack is seen by some as a source of controversy.

Although a symbol of national unity, for many the union jack highlights the social, political and cultural splits that exist between and within the countries that make up the British Isles

The flag was created in 1606, following the accession of the Scottish King James VI to the throne of England. As nation-states did not exist, it was not initially a national flag but rather a way to distinguish the King's ships from merchant vessels.

Gradually it was adopted as a national flag – by custom, rather than

By Sharon Norris

by an act of Parliament as is the case in other European countries.

However, although a symbol of national unity, for many people in the UK the union jack highlights the social, political and cultural splits that exist between and within the countries that make up the British Isles.

Even its official title is disputed. Purists (or pedants?) argue that the official title is the 'union flag' as a 'jack' is technically a flag on a warship, not to one used on land and in a time of peace.

The flag itself is an amalgam of the St George's flag and the Scottish Saltire. An additional red diagonal was added after the official union of Britain with Ireland in 1801.

Needless to say, a bone of contention for some Scots is that the

English flag overlays the St Andrew's Cross – in other words, England again comes out 'on top', while in Northern Ireland, the flag, which is used by Protestant extremists to underline their 'Britishness', is often seen as a symbol of sectarianism.

With Devolution leading to an increase in national pride in both Scotland and Wales, and the growing popularity of the St George's flag in England, some people question whether the flag now has any relevance. For Wales in particular, the flag is unrepresentative as, unlike Scotland and Ireland, no element of their flag is reflected in the union jack. Wales was already a principality of England in 1606.

Many have seen the promotion of a redefined concept of 'Britishness' – one that stresses the unity of all British people, regardless of ethnic or cultural background – as the way forward

---

Research undertaken as part of the recently-concluded ESRC research programme on Devolution seems to confirm this as it shows fewer people in Great Britain choose a British over 'local' national identity now compared with a decade ago, and that pride in Britain has fallen.

Nevertheless, while support for full-blown independence is up in Wales, where the Welsh Assembly has limited jurisdiction, in Scotland, where the Holyrood Parliament has much more extensive powers, it is on the wane.

In recent years too, within the context of increasing ethnic division in some parts of Britain, and the whole concept of 'multiculturalism' under attack, many have seen the promotion of a re-defined concept of 'Britishness' – one that stresses the unity of all British people, regardless of ethnic or cultural background – as the way forward.

Thus, it seems that there may still be a case for being British, and cause to fly the flag.
12 March 2006

⇨ The above information is reprinted with kind permission from the Economic and Social Research Council. Visit www.esrc.ac.uk for more information.
© ESRC

Flying the flag

Why flying the flag isn't just about supporting the team

As football fever sweeps England, with even Tessa Jowell flying an England flag from her Ministerial car, a University of Exeter sociologist claims these symbols have had a wider impact on national identity. Dr Anthony King points to factors ranging from flags on cars to major companies' sponsorship as creating a new national community with social bonds springing from sport.

Dr Anthony King, Reader in Sociology at the University of Exeter, has written about the social implications of flying England flags from cars since they appeared during the 2004 European Championship.

He says: 'In placing a flag on their car, people announce their support of the England team, but this statement is not an individualistic expression of personal pride. It is all about creating a sense of solidarity with other, mostly anonymous, people.'

The increased use of St George's cross itself is being widely welcomed by commentators as reclaiming the symbol from previous Far Right connotations.

Dr King adds: 'A potentially xenophobic British national identity expressed specifically by groups of young men in the 1970s and 80s has been replaced by a more localised English national identity, symbolised by the Cross of St George since the 1990s. This English identity is more inclusive, cosmopolitan and ultimately transitional than the former British identity. It encompasses social groups that were excluded before, going further to include women and immigrants, and is more open to other nations.'

He predicts the World Cup will have a positive impact on creating a national identity: Dr King says: 'The World Cup leads to an increased perception of a national community because it creates an opportunity for people to interact with each other on a regular basis within a charged atmosphere. The rituals surrounding sport are one of the most obvious ways that we can show networks building up to form a national identity.'

Major companies are exploiting these national solidarities to help sell sponsorship, shirts or sustain profits. The development of the England strip over recent years shows the transformation of English national identity in the era of globalisation with its increasing use of white and red and the St George's cross. Even the players' official suits bear the three lions prominently yet are made by Armani. Dr King explains: 'The England team's brand has drawn upon new transnational connections to maximise its competitiveness and attraction on the world stage.'

Dr King's ideas are expanded in a chapter 'Nationalism and Sport' in *The Sage Handbook of Nations and Nationalism*.

⇨ The above information is reprinted with kind permission from the University of Exeter. Visit www.exeter.ac.uk for more information.
© *University of Exeter*

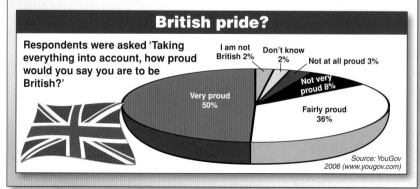

British pride?

Respondents were asked 'Taking everything into account, how proud would you say you are to be British?'

- I am not British 2%
- Don't know 2%
- Not at all proud 3%
- Not very proud 8%
- Fairly proud 36%
- Very proud 50%

Source: YouGov 2006 (www.yougov.com)

Study shows Scottish sense of 'Britishness' in decline

Information from the University of Edinburgh

People living in Scotland are more likely than ever before to say that they are Scottish – and less likely to say they are British – according to a new study into national identity in Great Britain.

A study by social scientists at the universities of Edinburgh, Dundee, St Andrews and Lancaster shows that more than eight out of ten people in Scotland see themselves as Scottish. There has been a long-term decline in Scots defining themselves as British, although most of this decline preceded devolution. And, for many people in Scotland, being Scottish is a far more salient aspect of self-identity than their gender, marital status and social class.

British national identity is still more commonly chosen in England (70%) than in either Wales (56%) or Scotland (59%)

At the same time as many as six out of ten people in England do say that they are 'English' but British national identity is still more commonly chosen in England (70%) than in either Wales (56%) or Scotland (59%).

These finding are among many from the most comprehensive study yet of national identity, funded by The Leverhulme Trust between 1999 and 2005. Eighteen new briefing papers have been published.

David McCrone and Frank Bechhofer who coordinated the study at the University of Edinburgh said: 'Two findings in our study have wide implications. Identity talk in Scotland and England is of a different order. National identity is readily and easily discussed north of the border, but in England, where local identity seems stronger, it is coded and implicit.

'Scots and the English do not have a common sense of being British. Imposing one is a policy which is unlikely to succeed.'

The study found that national identities in every part of the United Kingdom are multiple and plural. For example, of people in Scotland, almost half say they are both British and Scottish, and over a third in England and in Wales also have dual identities.

Looking at the impact of constitutional changes on national identity, the study found that people in England have little detailed knowledge of the changes, but are broadly positive or, at worst, neutral towards the Scottish Parliament and National Assembly for Wales. They believe that being English disqualifies them from holding strong views or even engaging in public debate on constitutional change.

Most English migrants to Scotland do not regard political participation in the new parliament as a way of 'becoming Scottish'. However, a small minority of long-term English migrants to Scotland make 'belonging' claims to being Scottish on the basis of a strong sense of commitment to Scotland.

The study found no evidence that constitutional change has affected the way in which people from Scotland are perceived or treated in England.

The success of the study has led to new funding by The Leverhulme Trust to explore how national identity in Scotland and England relates to issues of citizenship and social inclusion. This work begins in July 2006 and will last four years. The new study will carry out extensive survey work of a kind never done before, in Scotland and Britain. The study will pay special attention to Gaelic-speaking communities, both in the survey and carrying out fieldwork. There will be investigations into what people think, feel and do as regards national identity, using state-of-the-art experimental work in social psychology.
2 June 2006

⇨ The above information is reprinted with kind permission from the University of Edinburgh. Visit www.ed.ac.uk for more information.
© University of Edinburgh

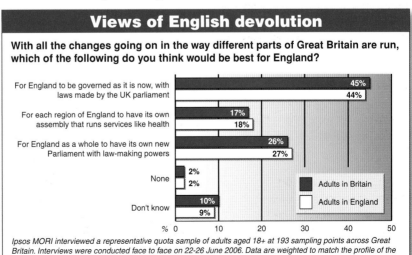

Views of English devolution

With all the changes going on in the way different parts of Great Britain are run, which of the following do you think would be best for England?

	Adults in Britain	Adults in England
For England to be governed as it is now, with laws made by the UK parliament	45%	44%
For each region of England to have its own assembly that runs services like health	17%	18%
For England as a whole to have its own new Parliament with law-making powers	26%	27%
None	2%	2%
Don't know	10%	9%

Ipsos MORI interviewed a representative quota sample of adults aged 18+ at 193 sampling points across Great Britain. Interviews were conducted face to face on 22-26 June 2006. Data are weighted to match the profile of the population.
Source: Ipsos MORI 2006.

Pride in Britain is on the wane

Information from the Economic and Social Research Council

Are we feeling a bit less British as a result of devolution? A recently completed three-year study analysed the impact of devolution on public attitudes and national identities in the four territories of the UK – England, Scotland, Wales and Northern Ireland. Findings suggest that devolution has made very little impact on our feelings of Britishness. 'Being British', however, is no longer as powerful a source of pride for the majority of the population as it used to be.

'Younger people are less likely to have acquired the strong attachments to Britain that older generations acquired in their youth'

'When we compare 2003 data with data collected since the 1980s, we find an unambiguous decline in pride in Britain with the percentage declaring themselves to be "very proud" of Britain falling from around 55 per cent in 1981 to 45 per cent today,' explains researcher Professor Anthony Heath. A generational reason is the most likely cause of declining pride in Britain. 'Younger people are less likely to have acquired the strong attachments to Britain that older generations acquired in their youth and have maintained throughout their adult life,' Professor Heath points out.

Significantly, pride in Britain has declined faster in Wales and Scotland than in England. However, this decline predates devolution. 'At this stage there is little sign that devolution itself has had any

E·S·R·C ECONOMIC & SOCIAL RESEARCH COUNCIL

impact on national pride,' he argues. Nevertheless generational change may well have implications for devolution. As older generations of unionists die out, the 'glue' holding the different parts of the UK together is likely to become weaker and there will be greater potential for independence movements to make headway.

Overall, devolution appears to have made little impact on national identity, except perhaps in England where it may have slightly strengthened an awareness of the distinction between English and British identity. If people in England are asked to choose a single national identity that best describes the way they think of themselves, slightly more now choose 'English' (39 per cent) and fewer 'British' (48 per cent) than a decade ago when 31 per cent described themselves as English and 63 per cent as British. In this study,

only 20 per cent of Scots and 27 per cent of Welsh opted for a British identity. While the overall levels of Britishness are clearly much lower in Scotland and Wales than in England, the extent of changes over time has been rather modest in both territories and appears to be part of longer-term trends rather than specifically affected by devolution.

Devolution itself, researchers conclude, seems neither to have brought England, Wales and Scotland nearer together nor driven them further apart. The much vaunted 'English backlash' against the 'privileges' of Scotland and Wales has failed to materialise. And support for independence in Scotland and Wales has neither fallen nor increased. Rather the broad contours of the current devolution settlement are broadly supported. 'Asymmetric devolution may be illogical, but it apparently reflects the varied contours of public opinion across the UK,' concludes co-researcher Professor John Curtice.
July 2006

⇨ The above information is reprinted with kind permission from the Economic and Social Research Council. Visit www.esrc.ac.uk for more information.

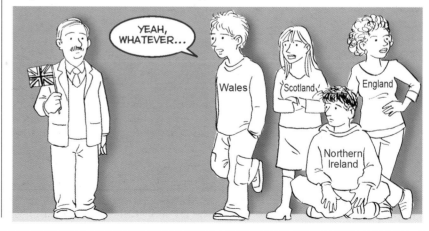

History lessons we should learn

Celebrating our national identity is pointless if we don't know how the past made us. By Tristram Hunt

The Chancellor's call at yesterday's Fabian Society conference for a celebration of Britishness should be cautiously welcomed by patriotic progressives. In an impassioned speech, he made the case for recapturing the union flag as a 'British symbol of unity, tolerance and inclusion'. But despite his best intentions, it is not supranational identities which Britons want to cling to, rather, the more particular identities of Wales, Scotland and, increasingly, England.

As a Scottish Chancellor of the Exchequer seeking to be Prime Minister of Great Britain, Gordon Brown has been making similar pronouncements since the mid-1990s. His empathy for and knowledge of the past are widely admired. Yet reservations creep in when the tub-thumping rhetoric drowns out historical analysis. For the Brownite virtues of Britishness – tolerance, fair play, liberty under law, an outward-looking mentality – are neither unique to these isles nor have they always been on display across Britain's long history. All too frequently, the Chancellor slips into a Whiggish narrative of national heroism which pays little attention to the less-becoming elements of our past. Many were dismayed when he chose a recent trip to Africa to celebrate the virtues of empire and demand we stop apologising for it. As academic Paul Gilroy rightly asks: 'When did we start apologising?'

Behind much of Brown's thinking is the canonical work *Britons* by Princeton historian Linda Colley. During the 18th century, she suggests, the modern British state was forged under the influence of empire, Protestantism and warfare. Seen in this light, Great Britain cannot be regarded as an ancient nation whose origins are lost in the mists of time.

Instead, it should be regarded as the specific construct of the Act of Union between England and Scotland. As such, it is a nation whose history extends not much further than the quintessentially modern national creation, the United States of America.

One of the most popular English icons – the cup of tea – is a microcosm of our imperial, global history of power politics and cultural exchange

---

Problematically for prospective leaders of the UK, the very forces which first crafted Great Britain in the 1700s are now in disarray. The ambition for empire is gone; Protestantism in its Anglican and nonconformist varieties is a shadow of its previous magnificence; and while the Prime Minister has done all he can to keep our martial spirit up, we are no longer involved in the kind of totalising military mobilisations of which the Second World War was the last.

The ties which bound Englishman to Scotsman to Welshman; the culture which celebrated David Livingstone, Florence Nightingale or Lloyd George as unifyingly British heroes has gone. So, according to Mr Brown, we need a new calendar of rituals and events to reunite the British ethos. Hence his call to convert Remembrance Day into British Day.

But at least since the early Seventies, what ever greater numbers have wanted to identify with is their national identity. Celtic nationalism emerged as a major political and cultural force during the Callaghan years and, through the demand for devolution, brought that government down. In the Nineties, English nationalism witnessed a wholly unexpected grassroots revival. On the left, the likes of Billy Bragg and Tony Benn championed the radical heritage of the English common man while on the right, Roger Scruton, Peter Hitchens and a small army of football fans rediscovered the symbolic meaning of St George.

Only last week, the government seemed to be encouraging such emotional patriotism. By launching the English Icons campaign, a website devoted to public expressions of pride in uniquely English products, Culture Minister David Lammy hoped to draw the sting of xenophobic nationalism and unashamedly celebrate the specific virtues of England. And if it is managed well, what this initiative could help the public realise is the long-established multicultural component of English identity. For one of the most popular English icons – the cup of tea – is a microcosm of our imperial, global history of power politics and cultural exchange.

Yet few of these ministerial initiatives will do much good unless we rethink our approach to the teaching of history and national identity in our schools. British Day will remain an empty initiative (like the Empire and Commonwealth Days of the Fifties), unless children are taught a far more comprehensive history of Britain. We need to be brave about teaching a rigorous, global narrative of British history and identity which goes beyond the obsessive heroism and victimhood of the Second World War.

If the union flag is going to mean something to Gordon Brown's future patriots, then they need first of all to know our 'warts and all' past.

15 January 2006

Ethnicity and identity

9 in 10 of Mixed group identify as British

National identity

In most non-White ethnic groups in Britain in 2004, the majority of people described their national identity as British, English, Scottish or Welsh. This included almost nine in ten people from a Mixed (88 per cent) or Black Caribbean (86 per cent) group, around eight in ten people from a Pakistani (83 per cent), Bangladeshi (82 per cent) or Other Black (83 per cent) group, and three-quarters (75 per cent) of the Indian group.

In most non-White ethnic groups in Britain in 2004, the majority of people described their national identity as British, English, Scottish or Welsh

---

People from the White British group were more likely to describe their national identity as English (58 per cent) rather than British (36 per cent). However, the opposite was true of the non-White groups, who were more likely to identify themselves as British. For example, over three-quarters (78 per cent) of Bangladeshis said they were British, while only 5 per cent said they were English, Scottish or Welsh. The non-White group with the largest proportion identifying as English was the Mixed group – 37 per cent identified as English and 52 per cent identified as British.

Country of birth

Among people living in Great Britain in 2001, the proportion born in the UK (England, Wales, Scotland or Northern Ireland) varied markedly by ethnic group.

Other than the White British group, those most likely to be born in

the UK were people from the Mixed ethnic group and from the Other Black group, 79 per cent in each. This reflects their younger age structure. A substantial proportion of the Other Black group were young people, who were born in Britain, and who chose to describe their ethnicity as Other Black and wrote in 'Black British' as their answer. Black Caribbeans were the next most likely group to be born in the UK.

Among the non-White ethnic groups the proportions born in the UK generally declined with age. For example, 83 per cent of Black Caribbeans aged 25 to 34 were born in the UK, but this fell sharply with age so that only 5 per cent of those aged 45 to 64 were born in the UK. For some other non-White ethnic groups (Black Africans, Chinese and Bangladeshis) this sharp decline occurred in younger age groups, reflecting their later immigration.

Sources

⇨ Annual Population Survey, January 2004 to December 2004, Office for National Statistics;
⇨ Census, April 2001, Office for National Statistics and General Register Office for Scotland.
Published on 21 February 2006

⇨ The above information is reprinted with kind permission from the Office for National Statistics. Visit www.statistics.gov.uk for more information.

© *Crown copyright*

Non-White groups were more likely to identify as British rather than English

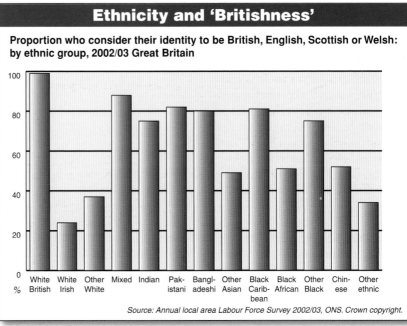

Ethnicity and 'Britishness'

Proportion who consider their identity to be British, English, Scottish or Welsh: by ethnic group, 2002/03 Great Britain

Source: Annual local area Labour Force Survey 2002/03, ONS. Crown copyright.

The decline of Britishness

An extract from *The Decline of Britishness – a research study*

Britishness in decline

As white people involved in the study were invited to talk about Britishness, many immediately and spontaneously changed the topic of the discussion slightly to talk instead about a perceived 'decline' of Britishness. This happened in all focus groups with white people. They attributed the decline to four main causes: the arrival of large numbers of migrants; the 'unfair' claims made by people from ethnic minorities on the welfare state; the rise in moral pluralism; and the failure to manage ethnic minority groups properly, due to what participants called 'political correctness'. Political correctness was said to be present at all levels of government in Britain (local, regional and national) and to be driven by the political and legal agenda of the European Union.

Most white participants were distressed by this perceived decline of Britishness. They felt victimised and frustrated, and many anticipated that social unrest would become inevitable. Much of their frustration was targeted at Muslims, rather than at ethnic minorities in general. Indeed, there were some indications that white respondents were drawing distinctions between ethnic minority groups.

The British Muslims in this study also felt victimised and frustrated. They resented what they perceived as being asked to display their 'loyalty' to Britishness and to choose between their Muslim and British identities. They felt that white people perceived a fundamental incompatibility between being Muslim and being British, while they saw them as compatible.

The future of multicultural Britain

White participants were largely confused about the notion of 'integration'. Most equated integration with assimilation. As they saw that people from ethnic minority groups

COMMISSION FOR RACIAL EQUALITY

had not completely assimilated, they then believed that people had simply refused to integrate, and that the project of multiculturalism had failed.

For ethnic minority participants, and for some white participants, integration was about participating fully in British society, while keeping alive certain parts of ethnic minority cultures

---

For ethnic minority participants, and for some white participants, integration was about participating fully in British society, while keeping alive certain parts of ethnic minority cultures. Those who shared this understanding of integration were generally satisfied with the current state of British society, although some questioned whether Britain's multicultural policy was able to support successfully the integration of everyone in mainstream British society.

The study shows that the main barrier to integration is not self-segregation by ethnic minority groups, but the subtle and everyday 'policing' of the boundaries of Britishness by white people and their demand for complete assimilation. These practices are not necessarily underpinned by racism, but they do serve to relegate people from ethnic minority groups, and Muslims in particular, to the margins of British society. These practices are mainly due to the implicit view (discussed fully in the initial report) that 'Britishness' is the prerogative of white and predominantly English people, rather than an all-embracing citizenship that includes different people. *May 2006*

⇨ Extracted from the Commission for Racial Equality's report *The Decline of Britishness – a research study*, conducted and written by ETHNOS for the CRE, and reprinted with permission. Visit www.cre.gov.uk for more information or to view the full report.

© *Commission for Racial Equality*

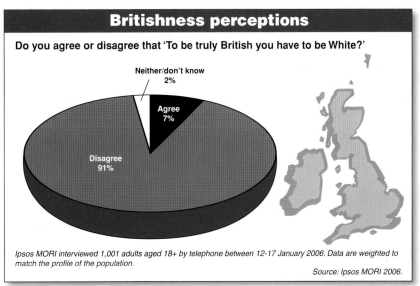

Britishness perceptions

Do you agree or disagree that 'To be truly British you have to be White?'

- Neither/don't know 2%
- Agree 7%
- Disagree 91%

Ipsos MORI interviewed 1,001 adults aged 18+ by telephone between 12-17 January 2006. Data are weighted to match the profile of the population.

Source: Ipsos MORI 2006.

Abandon multiculturalism to foster 'Britishness'

Multiculturalism has hindered efforts to build an inclusive British national identity, according to a Demos report written by Liberal Democrat Shadow Chancellor Vince Cable MP

Multiculturalism has hindered efforts to build an inclusive British national identity, according to a report published today by Demos, the leading democratic think-tank. Written by Liberal Democrat Shadow Chancellor Vince Cable MP, *Multiple Identities: Living with the new politics of identity* argues that Britain must abandon multiculturalism if it is to succeed in building a tolerant and inclusive sense of national identity. The report also proposes that Britain should introduce a managed approach to dealing with immigration based on the US Green Card system.

'Multiculturalism has detracted from the crucial task of creating a shared sense of Britishness'

'Multiculturalism has detracted from the crucial task of creating a shared sense of Britishness,' says the report's author Vince Cable. 'If we want to establish a truly inclusive and tolerant sense of British identity, we must abandon the myth of multiculturalism. Instead, we must build a tolerant national identity based on the concept of "multiple identity" – acknowledging that most of us "belong" to a number of different communities, whether national, ethnic, geographic or religious – combined with a strong commitment to the rights of the individual and law and order.'

The report examines the emergence of a new form of politics based on religious, racial and national identity, in the UK and across the

globe. It argues that UK policymakers must learn to deal with these forces in a way which protects individual liberties and a tolerant political culture.

'We have to learn to live with the politics of identity which promotes an open and inclusive society,' says Vince Cable. 'The threat to harmonious social relations in Britain comes from those who insist that multiple identity is not possible: white supremacists, English nationalists, Islamic fundamentalists. This is the opposition and they have to be confronted. An important element in that confrontation is the assertion of a sense of Britishness.'

The report sets out a programme of action to foster a new sense of Britishness, combining measures such as language requirements for new Britons with a commitment to upholding the rights of individuals and a strong commitment to law and order.

The report also sets out proposals to introduce a system of managed immigration based on economic need, similar to the 'Green Card' system operated in the United States. A new government body, modelled on the Low Pay Commission, would periodically assess the UK's economic need for new migrants. Cable advocates a system whereby quotas would then be auctioned to individuals or employers, building on the success of similar operations in the UK in relation to wireless spectrum and oil exploration.

The report will be launched on Thursday 8th September at Demos. Vince Cable will give a short lecture introduced by Tom Bentley, Director of Demos.

6 *June 2006*

⇨ The above information is reprinted with kind permission from Demos. Visit www.demos.co.uk for more information.

© *Demos*

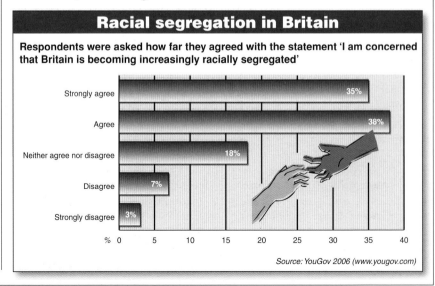

Racial segregation in Britain

Respondents were asked how far they agreed with the statement 'I am concerned that Britain is becoming increasingly racially segregated'

Strongly agree	35%
Agree	38%
Neither agree nor disagree	18%
Disagree	7%
Strongly disagree	3%

% 0   5   10   15   20   25   30   35   40

Source: YouGov 2006 (www.yougov.com)

Islamophobia and national identity

Rise in Islamophobia linked to perceived threat to national identity

Social psychologists at Royal Holloway, University of London, have carried out one of the first UK studies into the psychological reasons behind the reported rise in Islamophobia in the UK and how this is linked with a perceived threat to British national identity. Their research has shown that the more people feel that their country is under threat, the more likely they are to support more punitive policing strategies and harsher immigration policies, including policies which would reduce the civil liberties enjoyed by British Muslims.

A great deal of research has been carried out in the US following the 9/11 attacks, which suggests that our understanding of terrorism is largely dependent on media news stories about it, but until now there has been little research into these attitudes carried out in the UK.

This study, carried out before the 7/7 attacks on London, highlights the key role the media play in reporting acts of terrorism. The study shows how media articles portraying the idea that Islamic terrorism constitutes a significant threat to the UK can lead to increases in Islamophobic prejudice, targeted not just at Islamic terrorists, but all Muslims, especially those living in the UK.

The Royal Holloway team created two bogus national newspaper articles: one that suggested the continued threat of Islamic terrorism in the UK was high and one suggesting that the threat was low. The two articles differed in their portrayal of the likely consequences of terrorist attacks in the UK, with the 'high threat' article suggesting dire outcomes for the nation itself, and the 'low threat' article suggesting few long-term consequences for the UK.

Half the participants, all of whom were white British citizens between 18-30 years old, read the 'high threat' article and half the 'low threat' article, and then completed a questionnaire booklet containing measures of their attitudes towards Muslims and towards terrorism.

A further group of participants were allocated to a 'control' condition in which they read an article about crime on university campuses before completing the same questionnaire booklet as other participants.

Participants who read the 'high threat' article had significantly more negative attitudes towards Muslims, feeling, for example, that Muslims presented a greater threat to Britain's security, compared with participants who were in the control or low threat conditions.

The researchers also measured the level of British national identity that participants had, using a questionnaire scale. The findings revealed that those high in national identity had more negative attitudes towards Muslims, and showed greater support for the hypothetical immigration and policing policies compared with participants low in British identity.

Commenting on the findings, Drs Marco Cinnirella and Patrick Leman said: 'We know from surveys that since 9/11, British Muslims have reported increasing levels of Islamophobic prejudice and discrimination in the UK, yet there have been very few studies attempting to explain what lies behind this, or how it might be addressed.

'Simply reading a newspaper article about terrorism can elevate an individual's level of Islamophobic prejudice and lead them to feel more supportive of changes to policing and immigration policies that could restrict the civil liberties of British Muslims. Psychologically, we believe that these effects are partly driven by an individual's sense of British national identity, and the tendency to react negatively to anything that is seen to threaten the nation. Our findings also suggest that when such threats are perceived, negative stereotypes may be applied to the majority of British Muslims, not just those seen to be terrorists. We hope that in the long term, if we secure funding to continue this research, we will be able to look at possible ways to reduce these effects and combat rising Islamophobia.'
10 July 2006

⇨ The above information is reprinted with kind permission from Royal Holloway, University of London. Visit www.rhul.ac.uk for more information.
© Royal Holloway, University of London

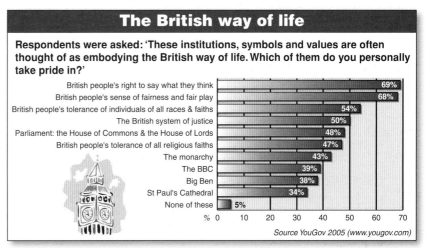

The British way of life

Respondents were asked: 'These institutions, symbols and values are often thought of as embodying the British way of life. Which of them do you personally take pride in?'

	%
British people's right to say what they think	69%
British people's sense of fairness and fair play	68%
British people's tolerance of individuals of all races & faiths	54%
The British system of justice	50%
Parliament: the House of Commons & the House of Lords	48%
British people's tolerance of all religious faiths	47%
The monarchy	43%
The BBC	39%
Big Ben	38%
St Paul's Cathedral	34%
None of these	5%

Source YouGov 2005 (www.yougov.com)

Citizenship test stumps one in three migrants

By Melissa Kite, Deputy Political Editor

A third of immigrants are failing the Government's new citizenship test amid complaints that some of the questions are too obscure.

New entrants must get 75 per cent of the 24 multiple-choice questions correct within 45 minutes to qualify for British citizenship.

> ### The test was introduced as part of the Government's efforts to ensure that new citizens show a commitment to the nation and its traditions

The test, which was introduced last November and is one of the last hurdles in gaining citizenship, has already created a new industry for consultants promising to coach immigrants through the process. There have also been claims of corruption, with one official allegedly sitting the test on an immigrant's behalf.

Of the 82,375 hopefuls who took the exam in the first nine months, 56,615 walked out with a pass while 25,760 failed, giving an overall pass rate of 68.7 per cent, the Home Office has confirmed.

The test (which includes questions similar to those in panel) was introduced as part of the Government's efforts to ensure that new citizens show a commitment to the nation and its traditions, rather than just a desire for a British passport.

A sample test on a Government website offers an insight into why so many immigrants might be failing. One question asks: 'What are quangos and non-departmental public bodies?' Another demands: 'What is proportional representation and where is it used?' Other questions include: 'How are judges appointed?' and 'How many young people are there in the UK?'

Others could best be described as trick questions. One states: 'In Britain, there is a well-established link between abuse of what substance and crime?' and then asks applicants to choose between drugs and alcohol.

Before migrants take the test they must study *Life in the United Kingdom: A Journey to Citizenship.* The book was subject to ridicule, earlier this year, when historians complained that it was riddled with errors – and even misquoted one of Sir Winston Churchill's most famous speeches.

A Home Office spokesman said: 'There is nothing to stop you taking the test as many times as you want, although we encourage people to go away and read up on the sections they failed, or improve their English, before re-sitting.'

Earlier this year, a college employee responsible for British citizenship tests was suspended after allegations that she helped applicants complete their papers as part of a test-fixing racket.

15 October 2006

Britishness posers

What percentage of the British population is under the age of 19?
A 25%
B 50%
C 5%
D 90%

What year were all women given the right to vote?
A They have always had the right to vote
B 1863
C 1952
D 1928

What is the largest ethnic minority in Britain?
A Chinese
B Pakistani
C Indian
D Bangladeshi

In the 2001 census, what percentage of the UK population reported it was part of a religion?
A 98%
B 75%
C 34%
D 5%

At its widest point, how wide is England and Wales?
A 75 miles
B 180 miles
C 1000 miles
D 320 miles

Answers: A, D, C, B, D

Immigration and community relations

Respondents were asked how far they agreed with the statement 'Current levels of immigration are making good community relations more difficult to achieve'

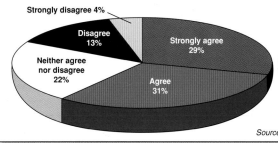

- Strongly disagree 4%
- Disagree 13%
- Neither agree nor disagree 22%
- Strongly agree 29%
- Agree 31%

Source: YouGov 2006 (www.yougov.com)

Identity cards

Facts and figures

By Andrew Bell

The history of ID cards in the UK

The carrying of identity cards was compulsory in the UK from 1939 to 1952. They were introduced as a security measure at the start of the Second World War and continued after the war to help in the administration of food rationing.

A consultation process carried out by the UK government in 2003 demonstrated strong support for the idea of an ID card with 79% of the public in favour, 13% opposed and 8% unsure

The police had powers to see identity cards in certain circumstances. If an individual did not show one when asked, it had to be produced at a police station within two days.

The National Registration Act, which made the carrying of ID cards compulsory, was finally repealed in 1951 following the change of government and an important court case.

In December 1950 Clarence Henry Willcock, the manager of a dry-cleaning firm, refused to show his identity card when asked to by the police following a minor motoring offence. Two days later, having failed to produce it at a police station, he was charged. In the magistrates' court he argued that it was wrong for the authorities to continue to use a power given during a national emergency when that emergency no longer existed. He was convicted but given an absolute discharge.

He appealed against the conviction and in June 1951 the case reached the High Court where the Lord Chief Justice concluded that the Act was passed for security purposes, and not for the purposes for which, apparently, it was now being used. This case hastened the end of the ID card in the UK.

Successful introductions of ID cards

Eleven nations in the European Union now have some form of ID card, even if they are not compulsory. Apart from the UK the only members without any form of identity card scheme are Ireland, Denmark, Latvia and Lithuania. ID cards have become widely accepted by their citizens. In France, for example, about 90% of the population carries one.

Failed attempts at introducing ID cards

The Supreme Court of the Philippines ruled in 1998 that a national ID system violated the constitutional right to privacy. The same happened in Hungary in 1991. In Australia, privacy objections came from the public and lobby groups rather than the courts. Massive protests against the Australian Identity Card in 1987 led to the withdrawal of the proposals.

Adding up the costs

The government claims that if it did not implement a scheme which covered everyone, but instead concentrated purely on implementing more secure passports and driving licences including biometrics, the 10-year cost of passports would rise to around £73 and driving licences to around £69. Under the national identity cards scheme, they estimate that:

⇨ a 10-year plain identity card would cost most people in the order of £35;

⇨ a combined passport/identity card would cost £77; and a combined driving licence/identity card would cost £73.

UK public opinion

A consultation process carried out by the UK government in 2003 demonstrated strong support for the idea of an ID card with 79% of the public in favour, 13% opposed and 8% unsure.

The results of a consultation carried out in 2004, however, based on a smaller response rate, were a lot

less positive towards the idea. In this survey, 48% opposed the proposals, 31% were in favour and a further 8% supported the idea in principle but with reservations.

Respondents in the 2004 consultation process who were supportive of the introduction of identity cards believed they would benefit society in a number of ways:

⇨ assist in the fight against crime and anti-social behaviour;
⇨ support counter-terrorism;
⇨ help in proving identity, particularly for those without a driving licence or passport;
⇨ help prevent illegal immigration and working;
⇨ make it easier for those entitled to services to access them and deter those who were not legally entitled to them;
⇨ provide proof of age;
⇨ provide a single 'all-encompassing card' that incorporates a number of existing documents, including the passport, driver's licence, proof of age card and national insurance record.

Those who were against ID cards cited the following reasons:

⇨ concerns about the security of information contained in the proposed Register (a centralised database) and 'function creep' (the increase of personal information held on the Register over time);
⇨ loss of privacy through a centralised register of personal details;
⇨ costs of the scheme;
⇨ accuracy of information contained in the Register national database;
⇨ concerns over disclosure of information held on the Register;
⇨ the scheme would aggravate racism by enabling police to disproportionately target ethnic minority groups;
⇨ worries over biometrics either because they would infringe civil liberties or because too much confidence would be placed in the technology/system;
⇨ ineffective in tackling illegal working and immigration because those who already employ with-

out National Insurance numbers would continue to employ those without identity cards.

The fight against terrorism

A study by human rights group Privacy International found that there was, 'almost no empirical research ... to clearly establish how identity [cards] can be used as a means of preventing terrorism'.

The report found that almost two-thirds of known terrorists operate under their true identity. Most of the September 11th hijackers were travelling under their own names and didn't have criminal records.

The remaining third use forgeries or impersonation to create fake identities, and high-quality ID cards would still prove forgeable.

⇨ The above information is reprinted with kind permission from the Citizenship Foundation. For more information on this and other issues, please visit www. citizenshipfoundation.org.uk

© Citizenship Foundation

Immigration

Respondents were asked how far they agreed or disagreed with the following statements:

I am concerned that Britain is losing its own culture.

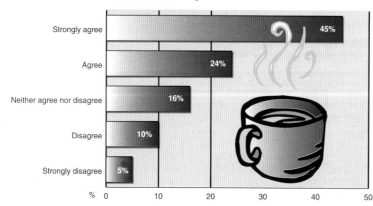

Strongly agree	45%
Agree	24%
Neither agree nor disagree	16%
Disagree	10%
Strongly disagree	5%

% 0 10 20 30 40 50

Many of my friends are immigrants.

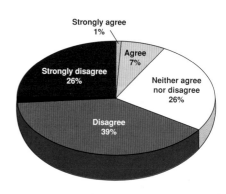

Strongly agree 1%
Agree 7%
Strongly disagree 26%
Neither agree nor disagree 26%
Disagree 39%

Amongst my circle of friends and acquaintances there is a definite concern about the high levels of immigration.

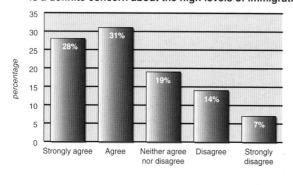

Strongly agree	28%
Agree	31%
Neither agree nor disagree	19%
Disagree	14%
Strongly disagree	7%

There must be an annual limit to the number of immigrants allowed to come to Britain.

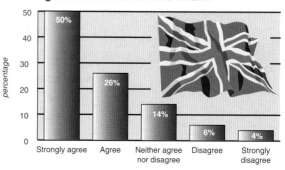

Strongly agree	50%
Agree	26%
Neither agree nor disagree	14%
Disagree	6%
Strongly disagree	4%

Source: YouGov 2006 (www.yougov.com)

Parliament

Information from the National Youth Agency

The House of Commons

The House of Commons is the main house in Parliament and is the central platform for MPs to do political battle. A Government can only remain in office for as long as it has the support of a majority in the House of Commons. Elected MPs from all parties debate new legislation as part of the process of making an Act of Parliament, and the Commons has priority over the non-elected House of Lords.

The leader of the party that wins the majority of Commons seats in a general election is the Prime Minister and is called on to form the next Government. Tony Blair has been the British Prime Minister since 1997. He was re-elected in 2001 and again in 2005.

'Money bills', concerned with taxation and public expenditure, are always introduced in the Commons and must be passed by the Lords promptly and without amendment. When the two houses disagree on a non-money bill, the Parliament Acts can be invoked to ensure that the will of the elected chamber prevails.

The House also scrutinises the work of the Government – it does that by various means, including questioning ministers, including the Prime Minister during Prime Minister's Question Time (currently on Wednesdays starting at 12 noon), and through a committee system.

Parliamentary discussions

All the discussions in Parliament, and all the written questions and answers between Members of Parliament, Lords and Ministers are recorded in the official record *Hansard*. TheyWorkForYou.com makes it easy to find out what is in *Hansard*'s record searching by who said it, when it was said, or what they were talking about.

The House of Lords

The House of Lords is the second chamber of the UK Houses of Parliament. Members of the House of Lords (known as 'peers') consist of Lords Spiritual (senior bishops) and Lords Temporal (lay peers). Law Lords (senior judges) also sit as Lords Temporal. Members of the House of Lords are not elected. Originally, they were drawn from the various groups of senior and influential nobility in Britain, who advised the monarch throughout the country's early history.

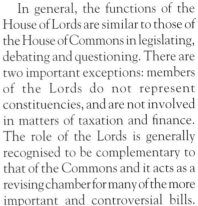

In general, the functions of the House of Lords are similar to those of the House of Commons in legislating, debating and questioning. There are two important exceptions: members of the Lords do not represent constituencies, and are not involved in matters of taxation and finance. The role of the Lords is generally recognised to be complementary to that of the Commons and it acts as a revising chamber for many of the more important and controversial bills.

The power of the House of Lords has diminished over the years. It was once very powerful. Following the House of Lords Act 1999 there are only 92 peers who sit by virtue of hereditary peerage. The majority of members are now life peers and the Government has been consulting on proposals and attempting to legislate for further reform of the Lords.

There were 731 peers in total on 1st July 2005.

European elections

An election is held every five years to elect Members of the European Parliament (MEPs) from the 15 countries that make up the European Union. The latest election was held in June 2004. A proportional voting system is used for this purpose in the UK. This means that in each region, each party won a share of the seats which roughly matched the share of votes each party got. Further information on European government can be viewed in the European Union section of www.youthinformation.com.

⇨ The above information is re-printed with kind permission from the National Youth Agency. www.youthinformation.com is the online information toolkit for young people from the National Youth Agency.

© National Youth Agency

Voting for dummies

So long as you know how to make a cross on a bit of paper, we'll hold your hand for the hard bit

Why vote?

Voting and elections are important parts of a working democracy. It's easy to think your vote won't count, but if nobody made the effort we wouldn't have an accountable government (one that answers to you, comrade, the people).

Can anyone vote?

No. You have to be 18 or over. You must also be a UK national. New legislation means homeless people, mental hospital patients (other than those with criminal convictions), unconvicted or remand prisoners and people who live on barges can all vote for the first time. Sitting peers in the House of Lords and convicted prisoners cannot vote.

It's easy to think your vote won't count, but if nobody made the effort we wouldn't have an accountable government

---

To vote, your name must be included on the register of electors. Avoiding registration is a criminal offence carrying a maximum fine of £1,000.

How do I get on the register?

The electoral register lists every UK citizen entitled to vote. It is updated every year using details from the registration form that everyone receives each autumn from their local council.

If you are unsure whether you're registered, call your local council and ask for the electoral registration office. They won't send you packing, club-style, if your name's not on the list. Instead, you'll need to fill out a form, which you can print off online.

TheSite.org

The form is a legal document, so it needs to be signed and returned to your local council. If you wish to complete a form but are unable to print it out, contact the electoral registration office at your local council.

I'm registered, how do I vote?

You should get a poll card about a week before the election. This will tell you how to vote, when and also where (usually a nearby school or community hall). This card is for information only. Don't worry if you lose it or forget it – you can still vote without it. It just makes it easier if you take it to the polling station and show it to the clerk there. He or she will give you a ballot paper that is stamped with an official mark.

The ballot paper will say how many candidates you can vote for. (In local elections you may have more than one vote; in parliamentary elections you will have only one vote.) Take the ballot paper to one of the polling booths and put a cross in the box next to the name of the candidate(s) you want to support.

DO NOT write anything else on the ballot paper, otherwise your vote might not count. Once you have voted you must fold the ballot paper to hide your vote. Then show your folded ballot paper to the clerk before you put it in the locked ballot box. You don't have to tell anyone who you voted for.

Voting by post

New arrangements allow anyone who is on the Register of Electors to apply for a postal vote at any election. (In Northern Ireland, a specific reason must be given and accepted before you can vote by post.)

You can ask for a one-off postal vote in advance of the election. Alternatively, you can request an automatic postal vote on a permanent basis or for a set period. Contact your local council for more information.

⇨ The above information is reprinted with kind permission from TheSite.org. Visit www.thesite.org for more information.

© *TheSite.org*

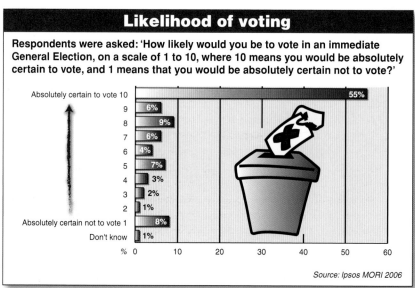

Likelihood of voting

Respondents were asked: 'How likely would you be to vote in an immediate General Election, on a scale of 1 to 10, where 10 means you would be absolutely certain to vote, and 1 means that you would be absolutely certain not to vote?'

Absolutely certain to vote 10 — 55%
9 — 6%
8 — 9%
7 — 6%
6 — 4%
5 — 7%
4 — 3%
3 — 2%
2 — 1%
Absolutely certain not to vote 1 — 8%
Don't know — 1%

Source: Ipsos MORI 2006

Election jargon buster

Information from HeadsUp!

When discussing elections and voting you'll come across bits of jargon and buzzwords. But never fear, the HeadsUp Jargon buster is here to help you get a grip on the lingo. Some of the terms you'll have heard a hundred times before, other words will be totally new...

abstention
not using your vote

activist
someone who volunteers to help a party get their candidates elected

age of electoral majority
shorthand phrase used to collectively refer to the minimum voting and candidacy ages

apathy
not being interested or willing to put in any effort – into voting for example

ballot
a vote

ballot box
the box into which votes are cast

ballot paper
a list of candidates standing in a constituency. The voter marks their choice by putting an X next to the name

candidate
a person who stands for election

canvassing
this is when party activists go around their constituency drumming up support for their party's candidate

constituency
an area for which an MP is responsible, usually made up of 60-70,000 voters (or 'constituents'). There are 646

democracy
a system of government where every citizen has an equal access to rights and responsibilities – including the right to vote

election
when people vote to decide on a course of action or choose someone for an official position

electoral register
the list containing the names of everyone who can vote

electorate
all the people who can vote in an election

eligibility
being allowed to do something, usually after meeting a requirement

exit poll
this is a poll that is made up of how people said they voted as they left the polling station

franchise
the right to vote

hung parliament
when no party wins an overall majority of the votes, Parliament is said to be 'hung'. The parties then have to form a coalition that will become the Government

landslide
term used to describe a party winning by a very large number of votes

manifesto
a declaration of a party's ideas and policies that it aims to deliver

margin
the amount of votes by which a candidate or party has won or lost

marginal seat
a constituency where no party or candidate has a clear lead

nomination
the act of suggesting someone for a position

poll
the process of finding out what people think by asking all of them the same question and recording the result

PPC
abbreviation of prospective parliamentary candidate

polling day
another way of saying election day

polling station
the place where people go to vote

recount
when votes are counted again, usually if a candidate isn't satisfied that the result was fair

returning officer
an official who is in charge of running elections in each constituency

safe seat
a constituency where a party or candidate has a clear lead over the others

The Houses of Parliament

seat
sometimes used to refer to a constituency or an MP's place in the House of Commons

soapbox
term used when people deliver a campaign speech

spoiled ballot
a voting paper that has been filled out incorrectly and cannot be counted

suffrage
using the right to vote

swing
when votes pass from one party to another

tactical voting
when voters use their vote not for the party they actually support but to keep out another candidate or change the shape of Parliament

turnout
the measure of registered voters who actually vote

vote
showing your support for a person or a thing

X
the mark that is made on a ballot paper by the voter

⇨ Information from HeadsUp! Visit www.headsup.org.uk for more information.

© Hansard Society

General elections

Information from Y-Vote MockElections

What's it all about?

This article is packed with all the information you need to turn yourself into an election expert.

Who decides when a General Election will be?

MPs are elected for a five-year term but the Prime Minister (head of government) can call a General Election at any time during these five years. An election is usually announced approximately six weeks before the polling day (when everyone votes) to give candidates a chance to get their election campaign going.

What is a General Election?

A General Election is an election that gives the people of the UK a chance to determine who represents them nationally in Parliament. Voters decide who to elect as their Member of Parliament (MP) and this MP will usually represent them for five years.

What happens when an election is called?

During election time, the MP is no longer acting as an MP but, if he or she chooses to do so, as a candidate campaigning to be re-elected. In each constituency there are candidates, usually from a variety of different political parties, campaigning to be the next MP. Candidates will usually be drawn from a number of different political parties all hungry for votes.

What do candidates do during a campaign?

All candidates undertake an election campaign to convince the electorate that they are the best person to represent them in Parliament. Campaigns consist of all sorts of activities including making speeches and debating with rival candidates. Another popular tactic is going 'door to door' in the constituency to meet potential voters and try to win their votes.

How many MPs get elected at a General Election?

There are 646 MPs in the House of Commons. Each MP represents a different area of the UK – these areas are known as constituencies. They are all similarly sized (approximately 70,000 voters) and each MP has a seat in the House of Commons. Another word for the eligible voters in a constituency is the electorate.

What is an election campaign team?

In the push to get elected, candidates must be well organised and have a hardworking team around them. This campaign team work to convince people to vote for their candidate. A few key positions in a campaign team are:

⇨ Canvasser: Canvassers must work very hard to talk to lots of people and convince them to vote for their candidate

⇨ Spin doctor: Spin doctors help show their candidate in the best light to the electorate and organise events like photo opportunities with local people

⇨ Press Officer: Press Officers act as a link between the candidate and the media and promote their candidate's good qualities and policies to newspapers and television.

What are parties?

In an election context, we are talking about political parties. People with similar views get together and in politics, they form parties. Members of the same party still can have differences of opinions on some issues but the majority of their policies will be similar. Most MPs usually belong to a political party, although there can be independent MPs.

Who can vote?

Almost every person over the age of 18 is entitled to vote. You are barred from voting if you are serving a prison sentence or a member of the House of Lords.

How do you vote?

Electronic voting is being tested and people can apply to vote by post (postal voting) but the vast majority of voters must go to their local polling station to vote. Polling stations are often set up in a local school hall and a vote is cast by placing a cross next to the name of your chosen candidate on a ballot paper. The day when everyone votes is called polling day.

Who organises elections?

The Electoral Commission (www.electoralcommission.gov.uk) are an independent organisation who oversee the conduct of elections and publish the results.

How do you know who has won?

MPs are elected under a process called first past the post. Put simply, this means that the candidate with the most votes wins the seat.

What happens once the election is finished?

The leader of the party with the most seats is asked by the Queen to become the Prime Minister.

⇨ The above information is reprinted with kind permission from Y-Vote MockElections. Visit www.mockelections.co.uk for more information.

© Hansard Society

A citizen's duty

Voter inequality and the case for compulsory turnout

Turnout and turnout inequality

Turnout in both national and local elections has fallen dramatically in the last decade – the 2001 and 2005 elections recorded the lowest turnout (59 and 61 per cent respectively) since the advent of universal suffrage in 1918.

As turnout has fallen, so the difference between the rates at which different groups vote has increased. Men and women vote at approximately the same rates, but older people and richer or better-educated people tend to vote in much higher numbers than young and poor or less qualified people. Some groups are now much more influential at the ballot box than others.

⇨ The gap between the rates at which the youngest and older age groups vote has grown consistently since the 1970s. While in 1970 there was an 18-point difference between the 18-24 age group turnout rate and the 65-74 age group rate, by 2005 the gap was 40 points.

⇨ 75 per cent of people aged 65 and up voted in the last election compared to only 37 per cent of young people. In other words, for every two older people who voted in the last general election, only one younger person voted.

⇨ Although there has been some decline in turnout among all income categories since 1964, the decline is most rapid for those in lower income groups. Moreover, whereas turnout increased in 2005 among better-off groups, it continued to fall among low earners. Whereas in the 1960s there was around a seven-point difference in turnout between top quartile earners and bottom quartile earners, this figure had increased to around 13 points in 2005.

⇨ Turnout at local elections has fallen by around a tenth since the 1980s, with the result that little more than a third of registered electors turn out to vote in most local elections. If anything, 'turnout inequality' is greater at local than national elections.

⇨ Many racial or minority ethnic groups vote at lower rates than their white counterparts, but race and ethnicity are not generally as important in shaping turnout behaviour as age or income/ educational attainment.

Turnout tends to be lowest in poor inner-city areas where there is a high proportion of young people.

⇨ Typically only about 80 per cent of the population are registered to vote in these areas, and even in national elections only around 40-50 per cent of those registered turn out to vote.

⇨ Taking Peckham and Camberwell, a typical inner London constituency, as an example, we estimate that roughly 40,000 people who could have voted at the last general election in that constituency did not vote – 58.4 per cent of all citizens. This is significantly higher than the official non-voting rate of 48 per cent.

Factors behind low turnout and increased turnout inequality

A range of factors seem to have combined to drive down turnout and increase turnout inequality. The relatively 'low-stakes' character of recent elections is perhaps the most important of these: the main political parties fought on quite similar platforms and in each case one party (Labour) was identified as a clear front-runner. At the same time we have seen:

⇨ Declining identification with political parties, especially among low turnout groups. In 1964 17 out of 20 people had at least a fairly strong identification with a political party. By 2005 the figure had fallen to less than 10 out of 20.

⇨ While interest in politics has remained steady overall, it has declined among young people and those from lower socio-economic groups. In 1994 there was a 10-point difference between young people's and old people's interest in politics but this had risen to a 25-point difference by 2003.

The 2001 and 2005 elections recorded the lowest turnout (59 and 61 per cent respectively) since the advent of universal suffrage in 1918

⇨ There has been a decline in a sense of political efficacy among low turnout groups. Young poor people are particularly likely to feel powerless. Whereas only four per cent of young people from the wealthiest households (above £50,000 earnings per year) believe 'it's not really worth voting', 15 per cent of young people from the poorest households (below £15,000 earnings per year) believe this (Park et al 2004).

⇨ There has been a gradual decline in the belief in the duty to vote since World War II. This decline has been particularly pronounced among young people in the last decade. In 1998 36 per cent of young people thought it was their duty to vote. By 2003 the figure had fallen to 31 per cent.

⇨ People are much more likely to vote if they are canvassed. But the decline in local political party and trade union activity, and the tendency for the parties to focus their campaigning on a small number of marginal seats, mean people are much less likely now to be canvassed than they were.

⇨ People are much more likely to vote if they live in a place where other people vote and expect them to vote – where there is an established norm of voting. There is good reason to think that this norm has declined in some areas – especially relatively deprived areas with high turnover and low social capital.

Tackling low turnout

A comprehensive strategy to tackle declining voter turnout and increasing voter inequality will need to work at many different levels at once. National and local government, schools, colleges, public services, voluntary groups and private businesses all have a role to play. Such a strategy will need to find ways of:

⇨ Further reducing poverty and exclusion.

⇨ Improving the standing of political parties.

⇨ Reinvigorating local political parties (perhaps through state funding for local political activity).

⇨ Encouraging civil participation and political deliberation.

⇨ Better supporting people who do get involved.

These, however, are ambitious and long-term measures. At the same time, relatively practical, easy-to-achieve reforms to the ways elections are conducted (including enforcing compulsory turnout) can make a substantial difference to turnout levels.

The following measures in particular can help boost turnout:

⇨ Weekend voting.

⇨ Encouraging and enabling electoral officers to take a more active role in promoting registration and turnout.

⇨ Making polling stations more accessible, by moving them to places like supermarkets.

⇨ Allowing people to register after an election has been announced.

A move to a more proportional voting system for Westminster and local elections is likely to have only a marginal influence on turnout levels.

Compulsory turnout

The most effective measure to increase turnout would be the introduction of compulsory turnout. Compulsory turnout is much more common than is generally recognised. Over 30 countries oblige their citizens to turn out for either national, regional or local elections, including Australia, Belgium, Greece and Switzerland.

Countries with compulsory turnout have much higher voting rates than those without it:

⇨ On average countries with compulsory turnout have 15 per cent higher turnout than countries where voting is voluntary.

⇨ Turnout in Australia has averaged 94.5 per cent in the 24 elections since 1946. In Belgium turnout has averaged 92.7 per cent in 19 elections since 1946.

⇨ Turnout inequality increased significantly when the Netherlands abolished compulsory turnout laws in 1970.

Though compulsory turnout is often known as 'compulsory voting', this is a misnomer. Countries with this measure do not oblige people to vote for a party or candidate, merely to turn up at a polling station or fill in a postal ballot form. Some countries give voters the opportunity to abstain formally, by including a 'none of the above' option on the ballot.

Compulsory turnout not only increases turnout, it also cuts down the cost of political campaigning and encourages the political parties to engage with those groups least interested in politics or most dissatisfied with the political system. Where turnout is voluntary, most political parties focus on motivating their supporters to vote, rather than winning the support of undecided voters. Where turnout is compulsory, however, parties can generally rely on their supporters turning out. This can reduce the cost of electioneering and/ or encourage parties to concentrate on winning over people who do not support any political party – people who often feel alienated from the political system.

Compulsory turnout does not violate any important liberties. Compared to some of the obligations the state imposes on its citizens, the obligation to turn out every couple of years is a very light one.

If compulsory turnout increases voting rates, it is not merely through threatening to punish those who do not vote, but through establishing that there is a duty to vote and upholding 'voting norms'.

Sanctions for failing to turn out vary. Some countries with compulsory turnout laws do not provide any sanctions against not turning out. Others impose modest fines. In Australia the fine for failing to turn out or offer a valid reason for not turning out is AU$20 – about £8.

Winning the argument for compulsory turnout

The little polling that has been done on the public's attitude to compulsory turnout suggests that people are divided on the measure, with about half the population inclined to support it and the other half opposing it. The public, however, has had little

opportunity to hear the arguments for and against compulsory turnout and their views are unformed. At the same time, politicians and the media could easily make political capital out of compulsory turnout, creating a caricature of those who support it as authoritarian or nannying.

The following could help test public support for compulsory turnout, win the public over to it, and help counter criticisms of authoritarianism:

⇨ Do further research on public attitudes to compulsory turnout – into how people think about and weigh the arguments for and against it. This will make it much easier to develop proposals in keeping with public values and attitudes, and, once developed, to win support for them.

⇨ Pilot compulsory turnout in a small number of local elections.

⇨ Create a citizens' assembly – a public inquiry conducted by ordinary citizens appointed at random – to explore the case for and against compulsory turnout and put forward recommendations in relation to it.

⇨ Undertake not to introduce compulsory turnout unless it is backed by a clear majority in a referendum.

Were compulsory voting to be introduced, government would have to monitor its development very closely, ensuring that sanctions for non-voting did not heavily discriminate against the very groups the measure is meant to support – those that currently turn out in very low numbers.

Compulsory turnout: our conclusions and recommendations

Over recent years turnout has fallen and the difference in the rate at which different groups turn out has grown dramatically. Some groups – mainly older and richer groups – now exercise much more influence through the ballot box than younger and poorer groups.

Compulsory turnout is the most effective way of addressing low turnout and high turnout inequality. A comparatively simple reform, it does not violate any important

liberties and it could probably alone reverse the trends of recent years and return turnout to post-war levels or higher.

Compulsory turnout is popular in countries that have it. The British public appears to have mixed views about it, with about half in favour of it and half against it.

Compulsory turnout can reduce the cost of political campaigning and/or encourage political parties to focus on winning the support of undecided and alienated voters.

For the above reasons, we believe the time has come for a serious debate on compulsory turnout.

We favour a system that would make turnout compulsory, while giving voters the right to endorse a 'none of the above' option on the ballot paper.

We believe that compulsory turnout should only be introduced if the public support it in a referendum.

We favour a system that would impose very modest fines on people who do not vote in national, regional or local elections and do not present a valid reason for not voting. Valid reasons for not voting would include being unwell, being out of the country, having to look after someone who was unwell, and having unavoidable work or family commitments.
May 2006

⇨ The above information is reprinted with kind permission from the Institute for Public Policy Research. Visit www.ippr.org for more information.
© *The Institute for Public Policy Research*

The Cabinet

Information from 10 Downing Street

What does it do?
The Cabinet is at the centre of the British political system and makes the big decisions about policy which affect us all.

Who is in it?
It is made up of senior members of the Government, known as Secretaries of State. Each Secretary of State represents a major Government Department, like health or education. There are currently 23 Cabinet members.

When and where does it meet?
Every Thursday morning when Parliament is in session it meets in the Cabinet Room of Number 10.

How did it start?
The modern history of the Cabinet began in the 16th century with the Privy Council who were a small group of advisers to the Monarch.

What role does the Prime Minister play?
The Prime Minister chairs the meetings, selects its members, and also recommends their appointment as ministers to the Queen.

What are Cabinet committees?
Much of the work of Cabinet is handed over to special committees. The Prime Minister decides who sits on the committees and what they are responsible for. Some of them only exist for a short period to deal with a particular issue.

⇨ The above information is reprinted with kind permission from 10 Downing Street. Visit http://youngpeople.pm.gov.uk for more information.
© *Crown copyright*

The myth of voter apathy

Low turnout caused by 'lack of trust', not apathy, survey shows

Political disaffection was by far the biggest factor behind the low turnout in the May 5th general election, a major national survey of non-voters shows.

The survey of 1,025 people who were registered to vote – but didn't – was commissioned by the Power Inquiry, a year-long inquiry into falling political participation including election turnouts and growing disillusionment with British democracy.

When asked to choose something that might encourage them to vote, most non-voters (54%) chose politicians keeping their promises and listening to people's views

---

Key survey findings show:

⇨ When asked to choose something that might encourage them to vote, most non-voters (54%) chose politicians keeping their promises and listening to people's views between elections (the figure rose to 72% for 18- to 24-year-olds – a group that are particularly unlikely to vote).

⇨ When asked the 'open' question: 'what was the main reason for you not voting on May 5th', 36% of non-voters cited political reasons which included a lack of difference between the parties and claims that politicians 'could not be trusted'.

⇨ Only 19% cited apathy as a reason for not voting when asked the same open question (see above). Only 1% mentioned the fact that the result of the election was a foregone conclusion as a reason for not voting.

⇨ 72% of non-voters said they were likely/very likely to get involved in a referendum when offered other ways of getting involved in political processes. 70% said they were likely/very likely to get involved in a meeting where they could set local council budgets with councillors.

Only 19% of non-voters cited apathy as a reason for not voting

---

⇨ More than 90% of non-voters identified three or more political issues that 'really mattered' to them despite the fact that 66% declared themselves as disinterested in politics – suggesting that many non-voters do not connect the issues that concern them to parliamentary politics.

Power Inquiry chair Helena Kennedy QC said: 'It is not good enough to blame low turnouts on voter apathy.

'People very clearly care about important issues – they just don't trust the politicians or the processes by which they claim their mandates. Above all, they don't feel that they have any real influence.'

The survey follows publication of last month's Power Inquiry report, *Beyond the Ballot*, which claimed that politicians lacked the will for changes needed to re-engage the growing numbers of people disillusioned with democracy in Britain.

Ms Kennedy said: 'Politicians have got to start giving people a genuine influence over political decisions. That means looking to new, more creative mechanisms which can really re-engage the voting public in British democracy.'
24 May 2005

⇨ The above information is re-printed with kind permission from POWER. Visit www.powerinquiry.org for more information.

© POWER

Voter turnout in General Elections

UK General Elections: electorates and turnout 1945-2005 (turnout = total valid vote as a percentage of the electorate).

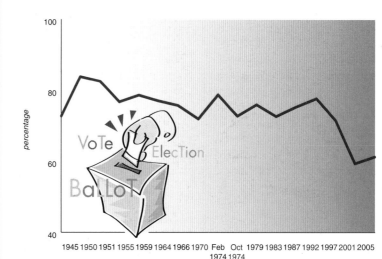

1945 1950 1951 1955 1959 1964 1966 1970 Feb Oct 1979 1983 1987 1992 1997 2001 2005
1974 1974

Source: The Electoral Reform Society 2006

Democracy and extremism

Do extremist parties have a role to play in our democracy?

When a Dutch court ruled in July this year that a party founded by a group of paedophiles would be allowed to stand for election, people everywhere quickly began to ask questions: if an obscene party like this could gain approval, what would be next? Had Dutch liberalism gone too far? What message would this send to other extremists and radical groups? The event sparked fierce anger from those who believe that radical organisations should be curbed, and has highlighted the fact that numbers of extremist parties may well be on the increase.

Whilst in theory the views and aspirations of parties like the PNVD (whose proposals include legalising child pornography and lowering the age of consent from 16 to 12) appear so outrageous that they could never gain approval with the public, the troubled events of the past tell a different story: less than a century ago, the NSDAP (Nazi party) was elected, fairly and democratically, enabling Hitler to rise to power and begin the systematic and horrifying process of exterminating millions of innocent civilians. Had a majority of the German population chosen to reject the ideas of the NSDAP, such atrocities would never have occurred.

Yet it is not only hindsight that can provide us with a stark and shocking warning. In September 2004 the British National Party, which propogates fascist and openly racist views, won its first council seat in the capital since 1993 with a landslide victory in an east London borough. Similarly the state parliament elections in Germany, which took place in the same month, saw the country's most overtly neo-Nazi party secure a footing in regional parliament for the first time in more than a generation. This offers worrying evidence that certain individuals, albeit a small minority, have failed to learn a lesson from the

By Nicola Whitehead

events of the past. But does it also mean that extremist parties such as the NDP in Germany and the BNP in Britain should be banned? The answer is no.

> **One must remember that even the views of the Labour Party were deemed 'extreme' in 19th-century Britain**

Whilst it is fair to say that the nature of democracy is changing, its fundamentals still remain the same: individuals in this country have the right to hold whatever political or religious beliefs they choose and to openly express those beliefs, and they are free to support and vote for an organisation that reflects their views. Given that Britain is a democratic country, individuals may deplore and speak out against parties with which they disagree, but they do not have the right to remove them from the political system. The same applies to the Netherlands; and so,

when the Dutch judge ruled that the Brotherly Love, Freedom and Diversity party (PNVD) should be allowed to stand in the next election he did so not because he endorsed its views but because an alternative approach would undermine the nature of democracy.

Arguably the extent to which far left and right political parties are truly democratic is open to debate. In February this year for instance BNP leader Nick Griffin went on trial accused of verbally stirring up racial hatred, and, though he was cleared of the charges brought against him, his trial did raise questions about the suitability of extremist parties in our modern democratic system. One must remember, however, that even the views of the Labour Party were deemed 'extreme' in 19th-century Britain.

When the Labour party formed, its principal objective was to campaign for workers' rights and to improve the living conditions of the working classes in the UK. For the upper classes dominating British politics at the time, as well as the large majority of individuals who felt that it was an employer's right to treat their workers as they pleased, these were considered to be radical ideals. Yet if the party as it stood at the time had been banned,

workers today would not enjoy the rights that are now taken for granted. Though it is unlikely that the views of the far right will ever become universally accepted, this example illustrates that people's ideas can shift significantly, and that banning a party now could prevent progressive change in the future.

It is fair to say that the nature of democracy is changing

Of course extremist parties can have a positive impact upon our democracy in other ways too. The three main political parties in Britain are often criticised for being too similar, particularly in light of Labour's shift further towards the right end of the political spectrum since 1997, and the result is that they fail to offer many members of the electorate exactly what they want. In order to propagate their views citizens are often forced to carry out a 'protest' vote. Take for instance the 2004 European elections: the UK Independence Party took nearly a 20% share of the vote, but this did not mean that 20% of voters supported the party above all others. Rather it confirmed that the public is sceptical towards further integration in Europe, and indicated to the government that much more needs to be done if Britain is to secure its place at the forefront of European politics.

Extremist parties are in this sense a fundamental aspect of our democracy, for they offer a means by which individuals can speak out against policies, while simultaneously raising awareness about the issues that actually matter to them. Were they to be outlawed these parties would pose a far more worrying threat to society, since banning an organisation rarely means that it ceases to exist. Instead many choose to campaign underground, and spread their message without anyone ever really knowing what they are doing.

The best way to tackle the rise in support for extremist organisations is to confront the problem at its roots.

Members of society need to be better educated, socially and politically, so that they can make informed choices about the kind of party they truly want to be supporting (be it a moderate organisation or an extreme one). Moreover if more were done to curb unemployment in areas where the problem is rife, then this would help to stifle feelings of resentment amongst some white citizens towards the ethnic minority population.
Nicola Whitehead is an intern for Unlock Democracy
8 August 2006

⇨ Information from Unlock Democracy. Visit www.unlockdemocracy.org.uk for more information.
© *Unlock Democracy*

How laws are made

Information from 10 Downing Street

We are governed by laws which tell us what we can and can't do in our everyday lives. Many of them have been in place for a long time.

Making a new law can be a long and complicated process.

A law is formally known as an Act of Parliament. Before any Government policy becomes law, it must first be written out as a Bill.

A Bill has to pass through many different stages in Parliament before it can be given Royal Assent and pass into law.

Ideas for new laws

Ideas for laws come from politicians, Government departments, interest groups or trade bodies.

The Cabinet decides what the priorities are for each legislative session. A session lasts about a year, usually starting around November.

The Parliamentary timetable only has room for a limited number of major Bills in each session, usually about 15-20.

Civil servants and Government ministers write the content of Bills.

A 'green paper' is then usually prepared to find out what people think of the ideas and to make changes if needed.

This is followed by a 'white paper' where the plans are given more details.

Passing a law

The Bill then receives its 'first reading' in Parliament, which provides a formal introduction of the idea to MPs.

During the second reading MPs get a chance to give their views on the plans. These debates usually last about six hours.

If the subject of the Bill turns out to be controversial then there may be a vote to see if it should proceed.

If MPs agree to the Bill proceeding, it then passes to 'committee stage', where a specially-selected group of MPs examine the proposals in greater detail. This stage can take up to several months.

They produce a report on their findings before the Bill returns to the House of Commons for its third reading and then on to the House of Lords for their consideration.

If a Bill clears this stage it goes to Buckingham Palace to be given the final go-ahead by the Queen.

Once the Bill has been implemented it is known as an Act of Parliament, and becomes the law of the land.

⇨ The above information is reprinted with kind permission from 10 Downing Street. Visit http://youngpeople.pm.gov.uk for more information.
© *Crown copyright*

Give citizens power to make laws, urges inquiry

Power to the People calls for radical power shift from centre

The biggest ever independent inquiry into British democracy today calls for citizens to be given powers to make and change laws, more powers for Parliament and local government and a radical new funding system which would allow voters to each allocate £3 of public money to the party of their choice.

The recommendations are among 30 Power Inquiry proposals designed to save British democracy from meltdown and tackle the creeping threat of authoritarianism by harnessing the kind of mass interest inspired by single-issue movements like Live 8 and the fox-hunting protests.

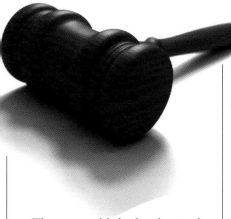

They are published today in the Inquiry's final report, *Power to the People* – the result of 1,500 public submissions and a comprehensive series of surveys and hearings held across the UK during the inquiry's 12-month investigation.

Power to the People says that millions are turning away from voting and parties to campaigning and alternative action because they have little influence over decisions affecting their lives.

Power to the People also calls for caps on party donations, reduction of the voting age and scrapping of election deposits as part of measures designed to plug the British public back in to democracy.

The 30 recommendations make up three major shifts in the way politics is conducted in Britain:
⇨ Devolution of power from central Government to Parliament and from the centre to local government.
⇨ Reform of the electoral and party systems so voters have more choice at election time.
⇨ Involvement of citizens in key decisions taken by politicians.

Headline recommendations include:
⇨ Two written agreements or Concordats should be agreed to redistribute power from ministers to Parliament and from central to local government.
  ⇨ House of Lords reform should be completed rapidly based on the election of 70% of its members.
  ⇨ On general election polling day, each voter should be able to allocate £3 of public money to support the local party of their choice.
⇨ The electoral system should be reformed to provide much greater choice and diversity at elections by giving small parties and independent candidates a greater chance of election.
⇨ Donations from individuals to political parties should be capped at £10,000, and organisational donations capped at £100 per member.
⇨ All public bodies should be required to meet a duty of public involvement in their decision-making processes.
⇨ Citizens should be given the right to initiate legislative processes, public inquiries and hearings into public bodies.
⇨ The rules on the plurality of media ownership should be tightened.
⇨ MPs should be required to produce annual reports and hold AGMs with their constituents.

Chair of the POWER Inquiry, Helena Kennedy QC, said: 'Politics and government are increasingly in the hands of privileged elites as if democracy has run out of steam. Too often citizens are being evicted from decision-making – rarely asked to get involved and rarely listened to. As a result, they see no point in voting, joining a party or engaging with formal politics.

'The old gentleman's agreement or conventions which underpinned our system are no longer observed. Parliament has had many of its teeth removed and government is conducted from Downing Street. A new written Concordat will reclaim Parliament's power by setting out the role of the Executive and elected MPs. It will make Parliament a place worth engaging with for those seeking change.

'Our political system operates as though deference to authority and allegiance to the two main parties still exists. But people have changed radically in the last fifty years. We have got to learn from the success of single-issue politics in capturing the passion of the public. We've got to tackle structural problems within the current democratic system so there is space for new political vision.

'Our report is about people having real influence over the bread-and-butter issues that affect their lives. We can only achieve that level of influence with popular debate and a genuine political will for change. That is why we today challenge politicians to rise above their party ranks and start treating democratic reform as a non-partisan necessity – not a political toy.'
27 February 2006

⇨ Information from POWER. Visit www.powerinquiry.org for more information.
© *POWER*

Young people 'feel excluded from decisions'

Information from Ipsos MORI

The latest Ipsos MORI Schools omnibus looks at the extent to which young people feel they are being listened to and understood for the Office of the Children's Commissioner (OCC).

It is important that young people's views are taken into account when making decisions which affect them so that policies and services aimed at children are designed with their views in mind. However, half of young people feel that they do not get enough say in decisions that affect them; only 18% feel that they do.

> **Whereas a quarter (27%) of children aged 13 or under feel that they do get respect and understanding, only 17% of children aged 15 and 16 agree**

Although we might expect older children to be given more of a say because of their age and maturity, children in Years 10 and 11 are actually more likely than those in Years seven to nine to feel that they are not given enough say in decisions which affect them (62% compared to 45%).

Respect has also become an important issue following the Government's respect action plan, which aims to reduce anti-social behaviour on the principle that, with greater consideration of others, community spirit will grow and anti-social behaviour will lessen. On this basis, it would seem to be important that young people feel valued by adults

so that they in turn respect other people. However, only a fifth (22%) of children feel that they are given enough respect and understanding by adults.

This appears to be a greater issue with children over the age of 14. Whereas a quarter (27%) of children aged 13 or under feel that they do get respect and understanding, only 17% of children aged 15 and 16 agree.

Technical details

The 2006 Schools Omnibus survey sample comprised 280 maintained middle and secondary schools in England. The age groups included in the survey are 11-16-year-olds in curriculum years 7 to 11. Each school was randomly allocated one of these

curriculum years, from which Ipsos MORI interviewers selected one class at random (using a random number grid) to be interviewed. In total, 91 schools participated and 2,129 fully completed questionnaires were obtained from pupils. Fieldwork for the study was conducted between 24 February and 18 May 2006.

Data are weighted by gender, age and region. The weights are derived from data supplied by the DfES and the Welsh Office.
13 July 2006

⇨ The above information is reprinted with kind permission from Ipsos MORI. Visit www.ipsos-mori.com for more information.

© *Ipsos MORI*

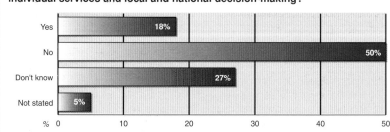

Young people and decision-making

Do you think you have enough say in decisions that affect you, for example in individual services and local and national decision-making?

	%
Yes	18%
No	50%
Don't know	27%
Not stated	5%

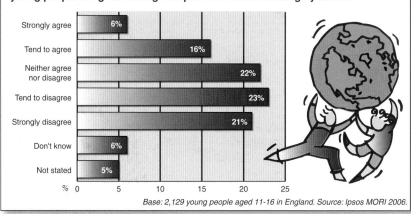

Please tick how much you agree or disagree with the following. 'Children and young people are given enough respect and understanding by adults.'

	%
Strongly agree	6%
Tend to agree	16%
Neither agree nor disagree	22%
Tend to disagree	23%
Strongly disagree	21%
Don't know	6%
Not stated	5%

Base: 2,129 young people aged 11-16 in England. Source: Ipsos MORI 2006.

Young people and mock elections

Young people vote Lib Dem in Y Vote Mock Elections

The Liberal Democrats have won the 2006 Y Vote Mock Local Elections, gaining 30% of the votes of the young people who took part. The Labour party and the Green Party were tied in second place with a quarter of the votes each.

The results, published today by the Hansard Society as part of their Y Vote Mock Elections project, supported by the Electoral Commission and the Department for Education and Skills, show a clear difference between the political attitudes of voters in the mock elections and their adult counterparts. The young voters revealed their support for the UK's third largest party, with the Liberal Democrats gaining nearly a third of school pupils' votes. Labour also found favour with the young people taking part, gaining 25% of the vote, as did the Green Party. The Conservatives' recent local election gains did not translate into a win in the mock elections, with them achieving 15% of the young people's votes. UKIP found favour with 5% of young people.

⇨ Lib Dem – 30%
⇨ Green Party – 25%
⇨ Labour – 25%
⇨ Conservative – 15%
⇨ UKIP – 5%

Approximately 100,000 pupils at more than 200 schools registered for the Y Vote Mock Elections which took place across the UK. The Mock Elections aim to boost young people's interest in politics by providing a unique opportunity to get involved in the excitement of a school election.

Students across the UK were involved in a range of election activities from standing as candidates, writing speeches and manifestos, and reporting for their school newspapers, to designing posters and building ballot boxes. As campaigns have drawn to a close in recent weeks, students have had a taste of voting in a live election.

The results show a clear difference between the political attitudes of voters in the mock elections and their adult counterparts

---

Michael Raftery, Mock Elections Project Manager at the Hansard Society, said: 'It's encouraging that over 100,000 young people registered for the Y Vote Mock Elections and engaged with the important issues that dominate local elections. Active involvement in elections helps young people to develop the confidence and understanding necessary for them to play a full part in both local and national political life.'

Beccy Earnshaw, Outreach Manager at the Electoral Commission, said: 'Young people have strong opinions and are hungry to have their say, but our research shows that they may be acquiring a habit of non-voting, raising the long-term possibility of a "generation No-X" of non-voters. The Y Vote Mock Elections are an opportunity for young people to understand how politics works, how they can get involved and why it matters, which we hope will help them develop the voting habit in the future.'

For more information on the Y Vote Mock Elections project, contact Michael Raftery: citizenship@hansard.lse.ac.uk
16 May 2006

⇨ The above information is reprinted with kind permission from the Hansard Society. For more information, please visit the Hansard Society website at www.hansardsociety.org.uk

© *Hansard Society*

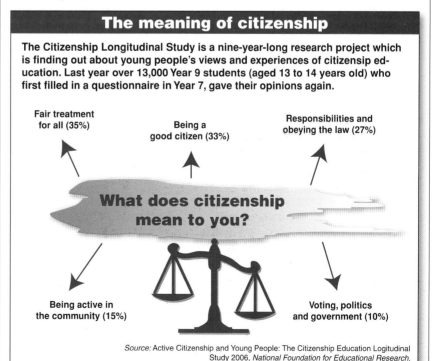

The meaning of citizenship

The Citizenship Longitudinal Study is a nine-year-long research project which is finding out about young people's views and experiences of citizensip education. Last year over 13,000 Year 9 students (aged 13 to 14 years old) who first filled in a questionnaire in Year 7, gave their opinions again.

Fair treatment for all (35%)

Being a good citizen (33%)

Responsibilities and obeying the law (27%)

What does citizenship mean to you?

Being active in the community (15%)

Voting, politics and government (10%)

Source: Active Citizenship and Young People: The Citizenship Education Logitudinal Study 2006, *National Foundation for Educational Research.*

Youth participation

Young people want to play a part in the running of their country – finds British Youth Council survey

Young people feel ignored by politicians yet still want to have more say over the running of their country, according to a major nationwide survey of young people carried out on behalf of the British Youth Council.

The British Youth Council are part of a growing coalition of organisations who are campaigning for the voting age to be lowered to 16. The issue is due to be debated at the Labour party conference this week after Unison joined calls for the voting age to be lowered.

Young people (aged 14-18) across the UK were surveyed to find out what they thought politicians think of young people, what issues matter to them and if they care about playing a part in the running of the country. Results showed that:

⇨ young people are becoming increasingly cynical about politicians' views of them; half of 14-18-year-olds (50.4%) think politicians see them as troublemakers and almost half (46.8%) said that politicians see their views as unimportant.

⇨ young people care about issues that directly affect them but also have views on a much wider range of issues. For example most are concerned about everyday issues such as their family or getting good exam grades and when asked what they would most like to talk to Tony Blair about, they highlighted issues such as facilities for young people, education, finances and giving young people a voice. But when asked what they would change about Britain if they were Prime Minister, they raised a much wider range of issues such as the war in Iraq and the relationship with the USA, the environment, public services, immigration and health and lifestyle.

Young people are becoming increasingly cynical about politicians' views of them

⇨ young people have strong views about current affairs and would be prepared to act on them. When asked if they would have voted if there had been a referendum on whether to go to war with Iraq, almost two-thirds (63%) said they would, of these 68.1% would have voted against going to war.

Dan Wood (aged 19), Chair of the British Youth Council, said: 'The results of this survey strengthen the case for lowering the voting age to 16 and challenge the commonly held view that young people don't care or know enough about politics. Young people want to have a say in how their country is run and they are clearly knowledgeable and mature enough to have strong views on a range of issues not just those which directly affect them.

'There is now massive support amongst a range of organisations and people, including many young people, who want to see Britain leading the way in promoting the rights of young people and a key part of this is being able to vote. Labour has already brought in a minimum wage for 16- and 17-year-olds and we'd like to see them press ahead with legislative reform to give 16- and 17-year-olds the right to vote. We hope that Labour members will support our campaign and back reform when the issue is debated as part of the democracy and citizenship debate at this week's Labour party conference.'

29 September 2005

⇨ The above information is reprinted with kind permission from the British Youth Council. Visit www. byc.org.uk for more information.

© *British Youth Council*

Votes at 16

Information from TheSite.org

Joseph Ammoun is 17, lives in Bexhill-on-Sea, and is studying Modern History, Politics, English Literature and Law. Joseph has been involved in the Youth Parliament (UKYP) for over three years and is its 'Votes at 16' Campaign Organiser.

Joseph argues that the voting age should be lowered to the age of 16 to give young people more of a say in how the country is run.

I recently finished my term as member of Youth Parliament for Hastings and Rother, an area which saw more than 3,000 young people vote in the UKYP January election. The new MYP (Member of Youth Parliament), like those before him, was voted into office with a greater number of votes by young people than most county councillors receive in elections around the country.

There's a great level of inconsistency about the age at which a person gains civil rights and responsibilities. At the age of 16 a young person can choose to finish education, leave home, join the armed forces, have sex, and start a family. In fact, if a young person is earning enough, they can even pay tax – and yet they do not have the right to vote or to have a role in deciding who will make law and govern the country.

Many adults believe that young people do not have a very great interest in voting or elections and that they'll drift into it later in life. However, the decline in turnout in recent years would suggest that this isn't the case; those who choose not to vote when they are young may never vote, even in general elections.

Not letting 16- and 17-year-olds express their political views through the ballot box, gives the impression to young people and to the rest of society, that young people's views are not valid and that they are not equal citizens. Lowering the voting age to 16 will give young people the potential to further influence and be involved in the political process, and help prevent the disillusionment felt by many.

Considering the role young people will play in the future prospects of this country and the number of issues our generation will be expected to deal with, I believe that the current voting age gives out a very negative message.

Many past and current members of the House of Commons benefited directly from the last lowering of the voting age in 1970. These include the Chancellor of the Exchequer, Gordon Brown, former Liberal Democrat leadership contender Simon Hughes and former Conservative Trade and Industry Secretary John Redwood. Who's to say that the next crop of leading politicians won't be turned off by the inability to have their say?

Experiments in Germany have seen a greater proportion of 16- and 17-year-olds vote than those aged 18 to 35 in municipal elections in Hanover. This shows that the new voting age could lead to a steady rise in turnout in general, particularly in the long term.

The youngest voting age around the world is 15, which is used in Iran

Just because some people have the opinion that the voting age shouldn't be lowered, I don't believe the case for votes at 16 is a lost cause. Although the Suffragettes campaigned for the right to vote to be extended to women, some women – and many men – stood against them, yet I doubt it would be possible to argue that women should not have the vote now. The same principle holds true for votes at 16.

The youngest voting age around the world is 15, which is used in Iran (for both men and women). A number of countries use the age of 16, including Brazil, Nicaragua, Cuba and Bosnia Herzegovina. Indonesia has a voting age of 17. Closer to home, the Isle of Man has recently passed a law bringing the voting age to 16 in all elections – the first place to do so in the British Isles.

The UK should now take the opportunity to lead the move towards an extension of the franchise to 16-year-olds and towards a society better adjusted to hearing the voice of its diverse population, just as we have done in the past.

⇨ Information from TheSite.org. Visit www.thesite.org for more information.

© TheSite.org

Voting age: reduction to 16

A timeline

13th century

From the 13th century, two knights are elected from each county by the county courts. They are soon joined by two representatives from the boroughs.

This is not obligatory and as representation in Parliament is originally considered a burden rather than a blessing, not every local community is willing to bear the expense of sending MPs to Westminster.

This results in gross inequalities in different parts of the country.

1430

By 1430 only owners of freehold land worth over 40 shillings a year are eligible to vote in county elections.

1542

Wales is now represented in Parliament.

1707

Scotland is now represented in Parliament.

1800

Ireland is now represented in Parliament.

1430-1832

In attempts to influence the make-up of Parliament, some monarchs extended the franchise in some boroughs, although the qualification to vote was often arbitrary.

In some, every male head of a household was eligible to vote, while in others it was restricted to the payment of local taxes or the possession of property.

Finally about one adult male in five could vote before the Great Reform Act of 1832.

1832

The Great Reform Act cleans up the corruption in the voting system. Every male who pays more than £10 a year in rates or rent can now vote. However, this only applies to the boroughs.

The 40 Shilling freehold (and a host of other possible qualifications) still applies to the counties.

The Act raises the electorate by 38 per cent, to 720,784 out of a population of over 10,000,000 of voting age.

1867

The Second Reform Act extends the franchise. Although this enables over two and a half million men to vote, it only applies to the boroughs.

This Act also denies the vote to anybody who had claimed poor relief in the qualifying period.

1872

The secret ballot is introduced. Before this, the entire community would be watching to see how people voted on polling day.

1884

The Third Reform Act equalises voting restrictions between counties and boroughs.

Over 50% of the adult male population can now vote.

Most British men above the age of 21 are allowed to vote as long as they have lived in the same place for a year.

1918, February

The Representation of the People Act gives the vote to women over the age of 30. It also reduces the time that voters must live in the same place from one year to six months.

1918, November 21

A Bill is passed making women eligible to be Members of Parliament.

1928

The Equal Franchise Act lowers the voting age for women to 21.

1969

The voting age for men and women is lowered to 18. This takes effect from 1970.

1998, July 1

Dr Ashok Kumar introduces a Ten Minute Rule bill to debate empowering local authorities to consult with young people about services designed for their benefit.

2001, December 8

Matthew Green MP introduces the bill 'Elections (Entitlement to Vote At Age 16)' under the Ten Minute Rule. The bill is allocated a date for a second reading but runs out of parliamentary time.

2002, January 23

In Prime Minister's Questions Tony Blair tells MPs, 'I am not sure that we would always want 16-year-olds to do all the things they can do. I think that it [the voting age] should remain as it is.'

2002, November 27

Lord Lucus introduces the 'Voting Age (Reduction to 16)' bill in the House of Lords.

2003, January 9

The 'Voting Age (Reduction to 16)' bill has second reading in the House of Lords.

2003, February 27

The Electoral Commission announced the start of work on a review of the minimum age for voting and candidacy in public elections in the United Kingdom.

2003, Summer

A consultation takes place as part of the Electoral Commission's review of the minimum voting age.

2004, April 19

The Electoral Commission submits its final report to the government. It recommends that the age at which someone can become an MP (the 'candidacy' age) is lowered to 18. However, it does not recommend lowering the voting age to 16, saying there is insufficient public support for doing so.

⇨ The above information is reprinted with kind permission from the Citizenship Foundation. For more information, please visit the Citizenship Foundation website at www.citizenshipfoundation.org.uk

My voice, my vote, my community

Young people care about social justice but don't trust the Government to deliver it

A majority of young people want to influence Government decisions on social justice issues such as racism and opportunities for women but many also want to see more social control such as restriction on immigration and more punishment for young offenders. Fewer than half trust the Government to make laws that ensure people are treated fairly.

These findings are from a new study on citizenship by the Nestlé Social Research Council, with fieldwork amongst 11-21-year-olds carried out by MORI. The study shows their view of good citizenship is far broader than 'voting', with taking part in activities to benefit the community and the environment, and obeying the law ranking higher in importance.

Priorities for influencing Government

When asked on what kind of things they would like to influence the Government, social issues came high – such as healthcare (83%), better facilities for young people (80%), controlling crime (79%), racism (76%), drugs and young people (76%), the environment (73%), opportunities for women (68%) and controlling numbers of immigrants to Britain (64%).

National sovereignty also featured strongly with over half wanting to influence Government decisions on the effect of the USA on British politics (57%) and of the European Parliament on British law (55%). Only 15% agreed that we should use euros rather than pounds as our currency, with 64% disagreeing.

Less than half (48%) trust the Government to make laws that ensure that people are treated fairly whatever their background.

Social control

Responding to a question about contemporary social and political issues, the young people demonstrated a tendency towards greater social control with 51% agreeing that there should be more control of the Internet and 53% more punishment for young offenders. These findings contrast with fewer than two in five who would like to influence Government decisions about violence on television (38%). Their views on the legalisation of 24-hour pub opening are mixed with 37% disagreeing and 33% agreeing that this should happen.

Being a good citizen

Young people do not see voting in elections as the most important aspect of being a 'good citizen'. It comes fourth (at 67%), after obeying the law (90%), taking part in activities to benefit the community (73%), and in activities to protect the environment (69%).

Young people's view of good citizenship is far broader than 'voting'

Their broad view of good citizenship is reflected in action. 64% gave money for the tsunami appeal, almost half had taken part in a sponsored event in the last two years (46%) and nearly the same number (47%) are likely to work with an organisation or charity to help people in need in the future. More than a quarter (27%) had helped to organise a charity event or activity.

Many want to make their voices heard, with 35% having signed a petition in the last two years and nearly six in ten expecting to do so in future. Seven per cent demonstrated against the Iraq war.

Around seven in ten expect to vote 'in the future' in a general (72%) or a local (69%) election. However, when they were asked how likely, if they were old enough, they would be to vote in the 'next election' only

23% of the sample as a whole were 'absolutely certain' to vote and a further 20% are 'very likely'.

Those who say they are likely to vote in the immediate future are also more likely to take part in other civic activities, and they report being more upset by events in the news than the less likely to vote.

A quarter of young people, however, have taken part in no civic activities and have little expectation of doing so in future.

Girls and young women are more upset by what is happening in the news and are more likely to help people in need in their community and to sign petitions than are boys and young men. They also more strongly want to influence the Government on issues around health, providing better facilities for young people, drugs and young people, racism, opportunities for women and animal experiments.

Those who are currently more active, and who are likely to be in the future, are more likely to live in a community where there is a lot going on for young people, and to have helped in community organisations. They are also more likely to have experience in school of being involved in decision-making about rules and policy and being encouraged to make up their own minds.

Party support

Taking the sample as a whole, when asked who they would vote for, the Labour Party was the most popular, with 19% support, followed by 15% for Liberal Democrats, 12% for Conservatives, 5% for BNP and 3% for the Greens. But amongst those aged 18 and over and thus eligible to vote, the picture was dramatically different, with the Liberal Democrats first with 23% support and Labour and Conservative running nearly equal at 12% and 13% respectively.

The Research Director of the Nestlé Social Research Council,

Professor Helen Haste, says: 'These findings show us that worrying about why young people don't vote is only a part of the story. Many are actively helping their community and are vociferous in making their views heard. Taking a broader view of citizenship gives us a richer picture and more scope for encouraging young people to become involved. Too many are inactive, however, and the findings tell us that community experience, as well as a democratic school climate, can do much.'

The study was conducted by the Nestlé Social Research Council in collaboration with the Economic and Social Research Council.
October 2005

⇨ The above information is reprinted with kind permission from the Nestlé Social Research Council. Visit www.spreckley.co.uk/nestle for more information.

© *Nestlé Social Research Council*

My voice, my vote, my community

Statistics from *My Voice, My Vote, My Community*, **by the Nestlé Social Research Programme**

Voting intention: how likely would you be to vote in the next general election?

Who do they say they would vote for?

Voting intentions: to what extent do you think you will be likely or unlikely to do each of the following in future?

Making one's voice heard: to what extent do you think you will be likely or unlikely to do each of the following in future?

Source: Nestlé, 2005

Youth parliaments and councils

Information from the National Youth Agency

Youth councils

The idea of youth participation in the political decision-making process is nothing new, but in the last decade, local youth councils have gained in recognition, popularity and influence.

Different approaches are taken in different areas – there are rural and urban models of how a youth council should be; single-issue groupings on housing or health for example; shadow councils and other forums in which young people participate.

Although there are many different formats, there are some features that all youth councils have:

⇨ it has to be democratic – young people representing others and not just voicing their own concerns;

⇨ it has to have access to power – to the committees and structures which make the decisions;

⇨ it has to be able to act on things which matter to young people and get results at its own pace.

The British Youth Council has developed a network of local youth councils enabling young people to have a genuine voice at community level. These offer participants a practical way of expressing their opinions and experiences to MPs, local authorities and the wider community. If you would like to find out more about youth councils in your area, and how to take part, contact the BYC at the address below.

Youth parliaments

Youth parliaments work to encourage young people to participate in the political process, to provide a place where a young person's voice can be heard and an environment where young people's views are taken seriously and acted upon.

One example is the young people's parliament in Birmingham. It believes that young people have the potential to be responsible and intelligent citizens and that young people can offer many exciting and creative ideas to better our society. They offer young people a democratic platform designed to foster responsibility, enable views to be heard, and to achieve change.

> **The idea of youth participation in the political decision-making process is nothing new, but in the last decade, local youth councils have gained in recognition, popularity and influence**

If you would like to know more about youth parliaments in the UK or how to get involved, contact The UK Youth Parliament. The details are listed below. Young people living in Scotland can also contact Young Scot.

Organisations

British Youth Council
The British Youth Council is the representative body for young people aged 16-25 in the UK. An independent charity, run for and by young people it represents their views to central and local government, political parties, pressure groups and the media.

For details of your local youth council, including its Local Youth Voices initiative and for more information on Rock the Vote contact the British Youth Council.
Telephone: 020 7422 8640
Address: 3rd Floor, 2 Plough Yard, Shoreditch High Street, London, EC2A 3LP
Fax: 020 7422 8646
Email: mail@byc.org.uk
Website: http://www.byc.org.uk
European Youth Parliament
The EYP is an international, non-partisan organisation which seeks to increase young people's awareness of European issues, and provide a truly unique educational experience. National EYP Committees exist to promote the objectives of the EYP in their country. This is often achieved by organising various European events.
Telephone: 01993 709940
Address: Witney House, West End, Witney, Oxon, OX8 6NQ
Fax: 01993 709910
Email: eypintl@aol.com
Website: http://www.eypej.org/
National Black Youth Forum
The National Black Youth Forum is a national network of children and

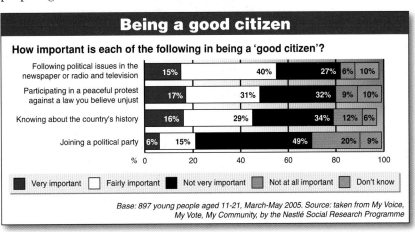

Being a good citizen

How important is each of the following in being a 'good citizen'?

	Very important	Fairly important	Not very important	Not at all important	Don't know
Following political issues in the newspaper or radio and television	15%	40%	27%	6%	10%
Participating in a peaceful protest against a law you believe unjust	17%	31%	32%	9%	10%
Knowing about the country's history	16%	29%	34%	12%	6%
Joining a political party	6%	15%	49%	20%	9%

% 0   20   40   60   80   100

Base: 897 young people aged 11-21, March-May 2005. Source: taken from My Voice, My Vote, My Community, by the Nestlé Social Research Programme

young people of Asian, African and Caribbean heritage. It encompasses the 12-25 age range and the organisation is run for and by these young people.

The aim of the organisation is to raise awareness about black young people's rights, how to access them and have them protected. They have written the Black Youth Charter in which over 200 black youth groups from around the UK have contributed. It is dedicated to all young people who have died through racist attacks and is available to order by email.
Address: PO Box 139, East Oxford DO, Oxford, OX4 1FT
infodesk@nationalblackyouthforum.org.uk
Website: http://www.nbyf.org/

School Councils UK
School Councils UK is an independent charity which promotes and facilitates effective structures for pupil participation in every school. Our vision is of young people as decision-makers, stakeholders and partners in their schools and communities.
Telephone: 020 7482 8917
Address: 108-110 Camden High Street, London, NW1 0LU
Fax: 0845 456 9429
Website: http://www.schoolcouncils.org/

UK Youth Parliament
The UK Youth Parliament is designed to provide a nation-wide forum for young people to communicate key issues of concern to political leaders, including members of the British government, the Scottish Parliament and the Welsh Assembly.
Telephone: 020 7219 5681
Website: www.ukyouthparliament.org.uk/

Young People's Parliament
The YPP is a Birmingham-based initiative, set up to help young people in the city to have a voice on everything that matters. The YPP now has a brilliant new home at Millennium Point, with a 200-seater auditorium where young people can meet to talk about issues and develop policies for making Birmingham a better place for the youth of the city. More than this, though, the YPP now provides a base for young people from all over the West Midlands, and will also be organising national and international events, bringing the youth of the UK together and communicating on a global basis.
Telephone: 0121 202 2346
Address: Millennium Point, Curzon Street, Birmingham, B4 7XG
Fax: 0121 202 2384
Website: http://www.bgfl.org/services/pupilwch/ypp.htm

Young Scot
Young Scot offers information and opportunities for young people aged 12-26 in Scotland. Also providers of the Young Scot Card – you can use it in over 1,700 outlets in Scotland, ranging from cinemas and theatres, to shopping, sports and travel. It's also valid at over 200,000 places in 38 European countries, since Young Scot is a member of the European Youth Card Association.

Visit the Young Scot web portal designed specifically with young people in mind, to cater for all tastes and interests. It's going to be an interactive and dynamic source of up-to-the-minute youth-related news and information, as well as crammed to the max with entertainment features, competitions, special offers, discounts, and the chance to get a free email address.
Helpline: Young Scot Info Line 0808 8010338
Telephone: 0131 313 2488
Address: Rosebery House, 9 Haymarket Terrace, Edinburgh, EH12 5EZ, Scotland
Fax: 0131 313 6800
Email: info@youngscot.org
Website: http://www.youngscot.org/
Opening hours: Info Line is open 12noon – 8pm Monday to Friday

Youth Parliament
Students across the country set the agenda, debate and vote online any time. Every student has equal opportunity to influence the agenda.

Operating continuously it produces a concise collective expression of student opinion on the issues of the day. The student voice in each school, constituency, county, country and for the whole UK can be seen at a glance.
Telephone: 01823 366000
Address: BigPulse Europe Limited, Suite F Castle Moat Chambers, Bath Place, Somerset, TA1 4EP
Email: contact1@bigpulse.com
Website: http://studentparliament.net/uk.php

⇨ Reprinted with permission from the National Youth Agency. www.youthinformation.com is the online information toolkit for young people from the National Youth Agency.
© *National Youth Agency*

Young politician

Would you spend the majority of your spare time campaigning for a political party? 21-year-old Henri Murison has been doing just that since he was 15. Here he explains what drives him to keep fighting for young people's rights – and why more of us should do the same

How I got involved in politics

I was very young when I got interested in politics, but I wasn't one of those people whose parents got them into it. The thing I really remember was in year 9 when we had a school election and I was involved in campaigning for Labour. I was lucky to have access to information about politics and to have inspiring people around. One of my teachers was a candidate in the election that year and that encouraged me to start having real discussions about it. I was already a Labour supporter, but it's quite a different thing to then go away and start thinking about joining a political party.

I joined the Labour Party when I was 15. I decided to go along to a local meeting at my local branch and it was really good – I met some really nice people, but not many young people, I must say! I got more and more involved and took part in a local campaign to get a Labour councillor. My local area is North Yorkshire – a very strong Conservative area. It was successful, which was great, but I do think what really got me to stick around was being welcomed and feeling like I was part of a network.

The way I see other young people

I think it's a bit of a myth that young people aren't interested in politics. Fair enough, we still vote in the smallest numbers and are less likely to get involved in political parties, but that doesn't mean we don't care. Young people are interested in politics in different ways. Not everybody is prepared to say: 'I support this party and I'm willing to go out and spend a significant amount of my time trying to get them elected,' which is fine: that's not necessarily for everybody. If, for instance, you're lobbying your local council about a skate park that's threatened with closure, that's just

TheSite.org

as political as getting involved at a party level. It's a mistake to draw boundaries between these. I've found that the reasons that young people get involved are actually very similar; it tends to be the same things that inspire people – they see something they don't agree with and they want to work out how to change it, or they want to feel proud about getting behind something they do agree with.

'I think it's a myth that young people aren't interested in politics'

I'm proud of what I believe in and it's not something that needs to be sold. I don't need to go to young people and say: 'look what we've done, aren't we brilliant.' A mistake that many people make is to think that political parties are only interested in getting people's votes. Obviously that is important, but in terms of building relationships, it's much better to know what people want and believe.

How I feel I've made a difference

I'm involved in the national committee of Labour Students, a student branch of the Labour Party, and I've been elected to carry on next year. It involves encouraging people to get involved, lots of organising and supporting other local clubs and groups.

When I was a trustee of the British Youth Council I was doing very similar work: running events, getting people to come along, but from a very

different perspective. It was less about party politics, and in fact a lot of the people there aren't really involved in politics at all. It's really good that there are places like this that aim to get young people involved on a much more general level so that if they're not associated with one party they can still find out about how politics affects them.

I also work closely with Young Labour and we do a lot of work pressuring the government on issues that affect young people. Now we've got a National Minimum Wage for the first time for 16- and 17-year-olds and that came from young people both in and out of the Labour Party campaigning. We do have quite a strong voice that we use to lobby parliament and it feels good to know that we are being listened to and that we can help to make a difference.

The fact there's now an Educational Maintenance Allowance is also a massive step forward and is one of the most positive things that has happened for young people, but there are other issues I care about too. For example, I'd like to see concessionary transport for young people – it's something I'm sure lots of other people believe in, but unless we get together to articulate these issues, nothing will change.

I'm staying around next year in a paid position in Young Labour, but beyond that I don't have huge aspirations to stand for parliament or make a career out of politics. There are so many other people I know that would be better at that. I really enjoy campaigning and I think I'll always be involved in the Labour Party as a volunteer, as I find it really enjoyable.

⇨ The above information is reprinted with kind permission from TheSite.org. Visit www.thesite.org for more information.

Schools poor at teaching citizenship, says Ofsted

**By James Meikle,
Education Correspondent**

Schools are failing to ensure their pupils are politically and socially literate despite the government's determination to make citizenship lessons a key weapon in the fight against extremism, the education watchdog Ofsted warns today.

Progress is slow in helping pupils understand issues such as legal and human rights, central and local government, the electoral system and diversity, it says.

Schools are failing to ensure their pupils are politically and socially literate

The subject has been compulsory in secondary schools in England since 2002 but only a minority of schools have embraced the subject with enthusiasm, while a quarter of schools inspected in the past year were judged 'inadequate' for the quality of their lessons in citizenship.

The verdict comes as ministers step up the debate about Britishness and the rights and responsibilities of individuals and governments.

Ofsted says things are improving despite wide variations. In many schools there is 'insufficient reference to local, national or international issues of the day and how politicians deal with them'.

Ofsted's report says citizenship is usually taught best in its own right, rather than as part of a personal, social and health education programme (PSHE) or in a cross-curricular fashion with elements included in subjects like history, geography or English. A review of the 11-14 curriculum is already under way and inspectors make clear more room will have to be found for citizenship.

Miriam Rosen, Ofsted's director of education, said last night: 'Citizenship is still seen as the poor relation of more established subjects but it requires teachers to be highly skilled and able to deal with contentious and sometimes difficult issues.'

Most teachers are non-specialists. They are unclear about the standards they should expect from pupils, although this is changing. Dull or irrelevant teaching can be counter-productive, warn inspectors.

Standards are generally better in pupils' discussion than in written work, except on short GCSE courses. Ofsted recommends plans for full GCSEs and post-16 courses are implemented as soon as possible.

It rebukes schools that claim aspects of PSHE on family disputes or about bullying in drama are part of citizenship. PSHE, it argues, is about the private, individual dimension, including sex and relationships, drug education and careers guidance, while citizenship is educating children about public institutions, power, politics and community and 'equipping them to engage effectively as informed citizens'.

Pupils aged 11-14 should get about 45 minutes a week, say the inspectors, and 'the past four years have shown that where this time is found in bits and pieces, there is little impact'.

But the Department for Education and Skills says citizenship is still a relatively new subject and it is confident it will continue to improve.

28 September 2006
© *Guardian Newspapers Limited 2006*

Citizenship education

Citizenship education became a statutory national curriculum subject in secondary schools in September 2002. The Citizenship and Personal, Social and Health Education framework was introduced into primary schools in 2000.

Citizenship education has three strands:
⇨ social and moral responsibility: pupils learn, from the beginning, self-confidence and socially and morally responsible behaviour, both in and beyond the classroom, towards those in authority and each other;
⇨ community involvement: pupils learn how to become helpfully involved in the life and concerns of their neighbourhood and communities, including learning through community involvement and service;
⇨ political literacy: pupils learn about the institutions, issues, problems and practices of our democracy and how citizens can make themselves effective in public life, locally, regionally, and nationally, through skills as well as knowledge.

Citizenship gives pupils the knowledge, skills and understanding to play an effective role in society. It helps them to become informed, thoughtful and responsible citizens aware of duties and rights. It promotes their spiritual, moral, social and cultural development, making them more self-confident. It encourages pupils to play a helpful part in the life of their school, community and world.

⇨ The above information is reprinted with kind permission from Teachernet. Visit www.teachernet.gov.uk for more information.
© *Crown copyright*

What is Global Citizenship?

Information from Oxfam

You may well have come across the notion of 'Global Citizenship', but what does it mean? It is a term being used increasingly in educational circles, and consequently there are a variety of views about what it is. These range from the idea that everyone is a citizen of the globe to the standpoint that in a legal sense there is no such thing as a Global Citizen.

At Oxfam Education, we believe that Global Citizenship is more than the sum of its parts. It goes beyond simply knowing that we are citizens of the globe to an acknowledgement of our responsibilities both to each other and to the Earth itself. Global Citizenship is about understanding the need to tackle injustice and inequality, and having the desire and ability to work actively to do so. It is about valuing the Earth as precious and unique, and safeguarding the future for those coming after us. Global Citizenship is a way of thinking and behaving. It is an outlook on life, a belief that we can make a difference.

We see a Global Citizen as someone who:

⇨ is aware of the wider world and has a sense of their own role as a world citizen;
⇨ respects and values diversity;
⇨ has an understanding of how the world works economically, politically, socially, culturally, technologically and environmentally;
⇨ is outraged by social injustice;
⇨ participates in and contributes to the community at a range of levels from local to global;
⇨ is willing to act to make the world a more sustainable place;
⇨ takes responsibility for their actions.

(Oxfam 1997)

This description of a Global Citizen is the ideal. It may feel like rather a tall order, but don't be put off! Everyone has the potential to be a Global Citizen if they wish to, and

is somewhere along the path towards that goal. For those willing to take up the challenge, all you need is courage, commitment, and a sense of humour.

To create a world of Global Citizens, education must be a priority. Global Citizenship is not an additional subject – it is an ethos. It can best be implemented through a whole-school approach, involving everyone with a stake in educating children, from the children themselves to those with teaching and non-teaching roles in the school, parents, governors/school board members, and the wider community.

It can also be promoted in class through teaching the existing curriculum in a way that highlights aspects such as social justice, the appreciation of diversity and the importance of sustainable development.

In the wider school setting, Global Citizenship can be reflected in the way you relate to those around you: it is as much to do with how visitors are welcomed as it is about what and how teachers teach. This is because Global Citizenship in schools is based on the following principles.

⇨ The importance of reaffirming or developing a sense of identity and self-esteem.
⇨ Valuing all pupils and addressing inequality within and outside school.
⇨ Acknowledging the importance of relevant values, attitudes, and personal and social education.
⇨ Willingness to learn from the experiences of others around the world.
⇨ Relevance to young people's interests and needs.
⇨ Supporting and increasing young people's motivation to effect change.

⇨ A holistic approach to Global Citizenship – that it should be an ethos permeating all areas of school life.

(Oxfam 1997)

These principles apply throughout school life, across all subjects and within all age groups. We see them as the foundation on which education should be built: as a basic entitlement for all pupils.

⇨ The Oxfam logo, and material on this page, from http://www.oxfam.org.uk/coolplanet/teachers/globciti/whatis.htm is reproduced with the permission of Oxfam GB, Oxfam House, John Smith Drive, Cowley, Oxford OX4 2JY, UK www.oxfam.org.uk. Oxfam GB does not necessarily endorse any text or activities that accompany the materials.

© Oxfam

European Union citizenship

Information from Civitas

All people who hold nationality in any of the twenty-five EU member states are also EU citizens. This means that while they are citizens of their home country, with the rights and responsibilities that citizenship involves, they are also citizens of the European Union, with extra rights and duties. This can be a difficult idea to grasp. While it is fairly easy to understand how one is a citizen of a state, how do you define citizenship of an international organisation such as the EU? While certain key elements of EU citizenship are laid out in the EU treaties, wider questions exist about what it really means for the people of Europe. Can there be such a thing as a European 'identity' – do symbols such as the European flag actually help people to feel more European?

Citizenship has long been linked to national identity

History

The idea of EU citizenship was first presented in the Maastricht Treaty (1992). This 'resolved to establish a citizenship common to nationals of all [EU] countries'. To this end, it laid out a clear set of rights open to all nationals of EU member states and looked forward to a time when these rights might be expanded further. European Community residents had already been carrying a symbol of shared European identity since 1988 when the first burgundy-coloured passports were issued by all member states in an attempt to standardise travel documents across the area. In 1999, the idea of citizenship gained another boost, when the European Court of Justice (ECJ) ruled that EU citizenship should be the 'fundamental status of nationals of member states'. While the draft European Constitution (2004) said that EU citizenship would not replace national citizenship, it re-enforced the idea set out at Maastricht.

How does EU citizenship work?

The Treaty of Rome (1957) set out the idea of freedom of movement – that people should be allowed to move freely across national borders. The Maastricht Treaty built upon this principle and set out four rights that are open to all nationals of EU member states. These are the right to move and reside within EU territory; the right to vote and stand for election at local and European level in any member state; the right to protection from the diplomatic authorities of any member state when travelling outside the EU, and the right to petition the European Parliament.

However, the idea of being a European citizen goes further. It is part of broader attempts to forge a unified European identity. One symbol of this identity is the European flag (twelve gold stars on a blue background), which was adopted in 1985. The EU also has an official anthem, the 'Ode to Joy' from Beethoven's Ninth Symphony. Furthermore, 9 May has been declared Europe Day, which is marked by celebrations in some parts of Europe.

Facts and figures

⇨ 9 May was chosen as Europe Day because it was the date in 1950 on which the French politician Robert Schuman first proposed the idea of European co-operation that eventually grew into the European Union.

⇨ The EU has a population of four hundred and fifty-seven million people.

Arguments

For

⇨ Giving people EU citizenship gives them concrete rights that benefit everyone.

⇨ The idea of EU citizenship contributes to bringing the peoples of Europe closer together. This not only benefits the process of European integration, but supports peace and understanding across the continent.

⇨ Despite a history scarred by conflict, Europeans do have much in common and it is good to celebrate this.

⇨ The principle of European citizenship encourages people to move around the EU to study or find work.

Against

⇨ Citizenship has long been linked to national identity. An important part of the way in which people define who they are relates to the country in which they live. This cannot be transformed through a treaty.

⇨ European citizenship is meaningless – although there are broad similarities between the identities of European states, there are more significant differences.

⇨ The symbols of EU citizenship are a means of challenging the existing symbols of national identity.

Quotes

'The Union shall offer its citizens an area of freedom, security and justice, without internal borders, and an internal market where competition is free and undistorted.' Article I.10, Draft Treaty establishing a Constitution for Europe, 2004

'Let me say quite clearly that I can see no conflict between being a British citizen, a proud British citizen even, and a committed European. I carry a German passport and I am a committed European – and I feel no conflict.' Monika Wulf-Mathies, EU Regional Affairs Commissioner, 1995-1999

⇨ Information from Civitas. Visit www.civitas.org.uk for more information.

© *Civitas*

What do young people want from Europe?

Information from the Hansard Society

Latest HeadsUp forum survey suggests:
- ⇨ *55% say 'No' to the Euro*
- ⇨ *British first rather than European*
- ⇨ *Approved opening up Europe*
- ⇨ *Called for balanced EU reporting*

Under-18s made their voices heard in a Hansard Society online debate – 'The EU... what is its future in your eyes?' The forum ran from February 27 to March 17, 2006 at www.headsup.org.uk

Over a three-week period, the young people made four main pleas to decision-makers and to society in general:
- ⇨ 55% of participants pledged their support for the pound and did not want Britain to adopt a single European currency.
- ⇨ Most participants did not feel European. Many stated an allegiance to one of the home nations or Britain first, which was then followed by a diluted notion of feeling part of the EU.
- ⇨ Participants were full of praise for the EU for opening up Europe, giving excellent opportunities for people to broaden their horizons by travelling and working in other member states.
- ⇨ Participants made a direct plea to the media to report accurately and fairly on all matters relating to the EU. They said that this reporting contributed to misunderstanding of EU-related issues.

This forum has attracted online involvement from a record number of key decision-makers including relevant MPs and MEPs:
- ⇨ Douglas Alexander MP – Minister of State for Europe
- ⇨ Graham Brady MP – Shadow Minister of State for Europe
- ⇨ Nick Clegg MP* – Liberal Democrat Spokesperson for Foreign and Commonwealth Office
- ⇨ Eluned Morgan MEP – Labour MEP, Wales
- ⇨ Jean Lambert MEP* – Green MEP, London
- ⇨ Glenys Kinnock MEP* – Labour MEP, Wales

Most participants did not feel European. Many stated an allegiance to one of the home nations or Britain first, which was then followed by a diluted notion of feeling part of the EU

- ⇨ Tom Wise MEP – UKIP MEP, Eastern Region
- ⇨ Robert Evans MEP – Labour MEP, London
- ⇨ Christine Burton – from the UK office of the European Parliament

- ⇨ Gisela Stuart MP* – Member of the Foreign Affairs Select Committee
* *These parliamentarians provided a statement of support before the debate began and have been asked to respond to this report.*

Barry Griffiths, HeadsUp Project Manager, commented: 'This EU debate contained some extremely passionate and well-argued views on all sides of the EU debate. The fact that there is still such negative EU coverage in the media only highlights the dilemma that a lot of questions still remain unanswered around the Euro and not feeling European.'

HeadsUp is a vital resource for teaching the political literacy element of the Citizenship Curriculum. In addition to the forum where school students explore and debate the political issues and ideas that matter to them, there are teachers' notes, ideas for classroom activities and background information all available on the HeadsUp website (www.headsup.org.uk).
3 April 2006

- ⇨ The above information is reprinted with kind permission from the Hansard Society. Visit www.hansardsociety.org.uk for more information.

© *Hansard Society*

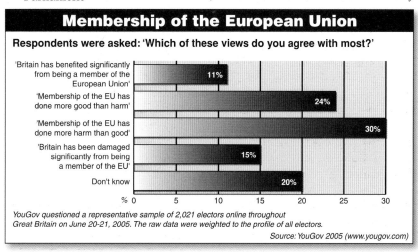

Membership of the European Union

Respondents were asked: 'Which of these views do you agree with most?'

View	%
'Britain has benefited significantly from being a member of the European Union'	11%
'Membership of the EU has done more good than harm'	24%
'Membership of the EU has done more harm than good'	30%
'Britain has been damaged significantly from being a member of the EU'	15%
Don't know	20%

YouGov questioned a representative sample of 2,021 electors online throughout Great Britain on June 20-21, 2005. The raw data were weighted to the profile of all electors.

Source: YouGov 2005 (www.yougov.com)

⇨ People who live in multi-ethnic areas and those with friends from different ethnic groups to themselves tend to have the most positive views about racial prejudice in Britain. (page 2)

⇨ Although a symbol of national unity, for many people in the UK the union jack highlights the social, political and cultural splits that exist between and within the countries that make up the British Isles. (page 3)

⇨ 50% of respondents in a YouGov survey described themselves as 'very proud' to be British, with a further 36% describing themselves as fairly proud. 11% described themselves as not very or not at all proud. (page 4)

⇨ People living in Scotland are more likely than ever before to say that they are Scottish – and less likely to say they are British – according to a new study into national identity in Great Britain. (page 5)

⇨ Pride in Britain has declined faster in Wales and Scotland than in England. (page 6)

⇨ In most non-White ethnic groups in Britain in 2004, the majority of people described their national identity as British, English, Scottish or Welsh. (page 8)

⇨ 91% of people surveyed by Ipsos MORI disagreed with the statement 'To be truly British you have to be White'. (page 9)

⇨ Multiculturalism has hindered efforts to build an inclusive British national identity, according to a report published by Demos. (page 10)

⇨ A third of immigrants are failing the Government's new citizenship test amid complaints that some of the questions are too obscure. (page 12)

⇨ The carrying of identity cards was compulsory in the UK from 1939 to 1952. They were introduced as a security measure at the start of the Second World War and continued after the war to help in the administration of food rationing. (page 13)

⇨ 45% of respondents surveyed by YouGov strongly agreed that Britain is losing its own culture. A further 24% agreed, while 15% disagreed or strongly disagreed. (page 14)

⇨ To vote, you have to be 18 or over. You must also be a UK national. Sitting peers in the House of Lords and convicted prisoners cannot vote. To vote, your name must be included on the register of electors. Avoiding registration is a criminal offence. (page 16)

⇨ Turnout in both national and local elections has fallen dramatically in the last decade – the 2001 and 2005 elections recorded the lowest turnout (59 and 61 per cent respectively) since the advent of universal suffrage in 1918. (page 19)

⇨ The Cabinet is at the centre of the British political system and makes the big decisions about policy which affect us all. It is made up of senior members of the Government, known as Secretaries of State. Each Secretary of State represents a major Government department, like health or education. There are currently 23 Cabinet members. (page 21)

⇨ When respondents were asked to choose something that might encourage them to vote, most non-voters (54%) chose politicians keeping their promises and listening to people's views between elections (the figure rose to 72% for 18- to 24-year-olds – a group that are particularly unlikely to vote). (page 22)

⇨ 22% of young people aged 11 to 16 surveyed by Ipsos MORI strongly disagreed with the statement 'Children and young people are given enough respect and understanding by adults'. A further 23% tended to disagree. (page 26)

⇨ Young people feel ignored by politicians yet still want to have more say over the running of their country, according to a major nationwide survey of young people carried out on behalf of the British Youth Council. (page 28)

⇨ A majority of young people want to influence Government decisions on social justice issues such as racism and opportunities for women but many also want to see more social control such as restriction on immigration and more punishment for young offenders. Fewer than half trust the Government to make laws that ensure people are treated fairly. (page 31)

⇨ Youth parliaments work to encourage young people to participate in the political process, to provide a place where a young person's voice can be heard and an environment where young people's views are taken seriously and acted upon. (page 33)

⇨ Schools are failing to ensure their pupils are politically and socially literate despite the government's determination to make citizenship lessons a key weapon in the fight against extremism, the education watchdog Ofsted has warned. (page 36)

⇨ 30% of people taking part in a YouGov survey agreed with the statement 'Membership of the EU has done more harm than good'.(page 39)

GLOSSARY

'Britishness'
There is currently much debate about British national identity: that is, what our values and identity are, or should be, and whether they are relevant in today's multicultural and increasingly global society. Many surveys have been carried out to discover how people would define 'Britishness'. Some things mentioned in association with the notion of 'Britishness' have been the Royal Family and Union Jack as British symbols, and pride, reserve and tolerance as British values.

Citizenship
A citizen is a legally recognised national of a particular country. 'Citizenship' refers to a person's status as a citizen, but is also a much broader term, encompassing the rights, responsibilities and duties of a citizen, such as social responsibility and voting in elections.

Citizenship education
Citizenship education became compulsory in secondary schools in the UK in September 2002. Students learn about social and moral responsibility, involvement in their communities, and becoming politically literate.

Citizenship test
Introduced in November 2005, this is a compulsory test, sometimes called the 'Britishness test', which migrants seeking citizenship of the United Kingdom must pass before citizenship can be granted. Recent evidence suggests one in three migrants currently fail the test.

Democracy
A system of government where everyone living in a country has a say in who runs that country, typically through elections.

Devolution
Devolution refers to the granting of governing powers by a central government to the smaller government of a state or region. In the UK, for example, both Wales and Scotland have had devolved governments since September 1997. These are responsible for legislation covering just Wales or Scotland, while central government covers legislation relating to all of the UK. Some people feel that England should also devolve.

Election
A vote which is held to choose someone to hold public office or other position. A general election takes place for people to decide which MP will represent them in parlia-ment. A local election is held to give people the opportunity to determine who represents them on the local council.

Extremism
When a political party has very extreme views and policies and sits at the far ends of the left/right political spectrum, it is often described as being an extremist party. The Nazi party which rose to power in Germany in the mid-twentieth century, for example, was an extremist party with far right views. On the other hand, the Communist party in power in Russia at that time was also extremist but to the far left. In the UK today, many would describe the right-wing British National Party as extremist.

Houses of Parliament
The British parliament buildings are the House of Commons and the House of Lords. Elected politicians are known as MPs, which stands for Members of Parliament, each of whom represent a constituency (an area of the UK), and who meet regularly in the House of Commons for political debates and decision-making.

Islamophobia
Islamophobia refers to prejudice against or fear of members of the Islamic religion. There is concern that negative attitudes towards Muslims have been increasing in Britain after high-profile acts of terror by militant Islamic groups such as Al-Qaeda.

Mock election
A mock election is sometimes held to assess who people would elect if they were to vote in a general election. These are most often held among young people under the age of 18 and therefore not eligible to vote in national elections, to gauge their political opinions.

Multiculturalism
Multiculturalism refers to a society which consists of a number of groups with different customs and beliefs, all with equal status. Some people believe that adopting a policy of multiculturalism in Britain, rather than promoting a British national identity among its citizens, has led to increased racial and cultural segregation.

National identity
National identity refers to the particular characteristics of people from a certain country, such as accent, dress or customs, and to an individual's sense of belonging to that nation.

Suffrage
Using the right to vote. The most common occurrence of this word is in the term 'suffragette', the name for members of a group in the late nineteenth and early twentieth century who campaigned for the vote to be extended to women – at that time only men had the right to vote in elections. This was finally granted to women over 30 in 1918, known as 'universal suffrage'.

INDEX

Additional Resources

Other Issues titles

If you are interested in researching further some of the issues raised in *Citizenship and National Identity*, you may like to read the following titles in the **Issues** series:

⇨ Vol. 121 *The Censorship Debate* (ISBN 978 1 86168 354 0)

⇨ Vol. 120 *The Human Rights Issue* (ISBN 978 1 86168 353 3)

⇨ Vol. 115 *Racial Discrimination* (ISBN 978 1 86168 348 9)

⇨ Vol. 98 *The Globalisation Issue* (ISBN 978 1 86168 312 0)

⇨ Vol. 94 *Religions and Beliefs in Britain* (ISBN 978 1 86168 302 1)

⇨ Vol. 92 *Terrorism* (ISBN 978 1 86168 300 7)

⇨ Vol. 89 *Refugees* (ISBN 978 1 86168 290 1)

⇨ Vol. 82 *Protecting our Privacy* (ISBN 978 1 86168 277 2)

For more information about these titles, visit our website at www.independence.co.uk/publicationslist

Useful organisations

You may find the websites of the following organisations useful for further research:

⇨ 10 Downing Street: http://youngpeople.pm.gov.uk

⇨ British Youth Council: www.byc.org.uk

⇨ Citizenship Foundation: www.citizenshipfoundation.org.uk

⇨ Civitas: www.civitas.org.uk

⇨ Commission for Racial Equality: www.cre.gov.uk

⇨ Demos: www.demos.co.uk

⇨ Hansard Society: www.hansardsociety.org.uk

⇨ HeadsUp!: www.headsup.org.uk

⇨ National Youth Agency: www.youthinformation.com

⇨ Nestlé Social Research Council: www.spreckly.co.uk/nestle

⇨ POWER: www.powerinquiry.org

⇨ Unlock Democracy: www.unlockdemocracy.org.uk

⇨ Y-Vote MockElections: www.mockelections.co.uk

ACKNOWLEDGEMENTS

The publisher is grateful for permission to reproduce the following material.

While every care has been taken to trace and acknowledge copyright, the publisher tenders its apology for any accidental infringement or where copyright has proved untraceable. The publisher would be pleased to come to a suitable arrangement in any such case with the rightful owner.

Chapter One: National Identity

Citizenship and belonging, © Commission for Racial Equality, *The citizenship survey 2005*, © Crown copyright is reproduced with the permission of Her Majesty's Stationery Office, *The union jack – a symbol of unity or division?*, © ESRC, *Flying the flag*, © University of Exeter, *Study shows Scottish sense of 'Britishness' in decline*, © University of Edinburgh, *Pride in Britain is on the wane*, © ESRC, *History lessons we should learn*, © Guardian Newspapers Ltd 2006, *Ethnicity and identity*, © Crown copyright is reproduced with the permission of Her Majesty's Stationery Office, *The decline of Britishness*, © Commission for Racial Equality, *Abandon multiculturalism to foster 'Britishness'*, © Demos, *Islamophobia and national identity*, © Royal Holloway, University of London, *Citizenship test stumps one in three migrants*, © Telegraph Group Ltd 2006, *Identity cards*, © Citizenship Foundation.

Chapter Two: Voting and Government

Parliament, © National Youth Agency, *Voting for dummies*, © TheSite.org, *Election jargon buster*, © Hansard Society, *General elections*, © Hansard Society, *A citizen's duty*, © Institute for Public Policy Research, *The Cabinet*, © Crown copyright is reproduced with the permission of Her Majesty's Stationery Office, *The myth of voter apathy*, © POWER, *Democracy and extremism*, © Unlock Democracy, *How laws are made*, © Crown copyright is reproduced with the permission of Her Majesty's Stationery Office, *Give citizens power to make laws, urges inquiry*, © POWER.

Chapter Three: Young Citizens

Young people 'feel excluded from decisions', © Ipsos MORI, *Young people and mock elections*, © Hansard Society, *Youth participation*, © British Youth Council, *Votes at 16*, © TheSite.org, *Voting age: reduction to 16*, © Citizenship Foundation, *My voice, my vote, my community*, © Nestlé Social Research Council, *Youth parliaments and councils*, © National Youth Agency, *Young politician*, © TheSite.org, *Schools poor at teaching citizenship, says Ofsted*, © Guardian Newspapers Ltd 2006, *Citizenship education*, © Crown copyright is reproduced with the permission of Her Majesty's Stationery Office, *What is Global Citizenship?*, © Oxfam, *European Union citizenship*, © Civitas, *What do young people want from Europe?*, © Hansard Society.

Photographs and illustrations:

Pages 1, 20, 31: Simon Kneebone; pages 6, 23, 34: Angelo Madrid; pages 13, 28, 37: Don Hatcher; pages 15, 29: Bev Aisbett.

And with thanks to the team: Mary Chapman, Sandra Dennis and Jan Haskell.

Lisa Firth
Cambridge
January, 2007